MERRIE ENGLAND

Merrie England.

BY

NUNQUAM.

DEDICATED TO

A. M. THOMPSON

(DANGLE).

LONDON

CLARION OFFICE, 4, BOUVERIE STREET, FLEET STREET, E.C.

WALTER SCOTT, 24, WARWICK LANE, E.C.

First published in 1893
Reprinted by the Journeyman Press, June 1976
97 Ferme Park Road
Crouch End
London N8 9SA

ISBN 0 904526 07 0

Printed in Great Britain by
Interlink Longraph Limited
45 Mitchell Street
London EC1V 3QD

PUBLISHER'S FOREWORD.

THE text of this little book first appeared in the *Clarion* during 1892-93 – the first working-class paper since the *Northern Star* to have gained a mass circulation and pay for itself. With some revisions and additions they were afterwards produced in volume form, selling at one shilling. As the editor of the *Clarion*, Robert Blatchford had already achieved fame amongst the paper's readers with his ability to write simply and effectively about the realities of nineteenth-century Britain and the necessity for Socialism. Such was his influence that the book met with immediate success, some 25,000 copies being sold.

In October 1894, the *Clarion* reprinted the same book at the lower price of one penny. As it contained 206 pages, and was printed by trade union labour, and on British-made paper, it could only be produced at a loss. This loss was borne by the proprietors of the *Clarion*. The sale of the penny edition outran all expectations. No one supposed that more than 100,000 would be called for, but in a few months over 700,000 had been sold, without a penny being spent on advertisements, and in the face of the tremendous opposition created by Socialist publications in those days. Later on an edition was published at threepence, and the total sale reached nearly a million copies. An American edition was said to have sold equally as well, and the book was translated into Welsh, Dutch, German, Scandinavian, Italian, Spanish and other languages, on none of which did Blatchford or the *Clarion* receive any royalties.

Merrie England's publication had come just at the right time, following hard on the heels of the formation of the I.L.P. in 1893. An indication of the effect it had on the British working-class movement was given by A. M. Thompson in his preface to Blatchford's autobiography:

> 'A year before its issue there were not 500 Socialists in Lancashire; twelve months after there were 50,000. A census taken at the time in a North of England Labour Club showed that forty-nine members out of fifty had been "converted" by **Merrie England**. As the *Manchester Guardian* lately said: "For every convert made by **Das Kapital**, there were a hundred made by **Merrie England**." '

It must be recognised that Blatchford's own brand of Socialism was in deep contrast to that of Marx. Its appeal was on the basis of ethics and commonsense; certainly not scientific. He himself never claimed to be a Marxist, yet his inspiration came, in the main, from William Morris – one of the very few Englishmen to have extended Marx's ideas creatively. In fact it was a pamphlet written by Morris and Hyndman that finally converted him to Socialism in the late 1880s, and it was undoubtedly from Morris that Blatchford learned the distinction which he drew so clearly in **Merrie England** between socialist and communist society – which he called 'elementary' and 'advanced' Socialism.

Blatchford was born in Maidstone in 1851 and brought up in the North. His mother apprenticed him to a brushmaker to avoid his taking up the same profession as his parents, both of whom were actors. But before long he had left his job and tramped down to London. With work difficult to find he decided to join the Army, and remained a soldier for the next five years. After returning to civilian life he became a timekeeper on the Weaver Canal, and during his spare time read as much as he could. This reading, and his earlier experiences, stood him in good stead when his journalistic qualities were recognised. By 1891 he was earning £1000 a year writing for the *Sunday Chronicle*, but within nine months was out of work because of his political convictions, and owing £400. On the resignation of his friend, A. M. Thompson, from the same paper, they decided with three others to launch the *Clarion*. It had attracted enough readers by 1895 to make it possible to move from Manchester to London and aim at a national circulation. With the development of the Clarion Fellowship, the name given to the numerous clubs which sprung up around the paper – the most famous being the Clarion Cycling Clubs – its influence reached a peak. Although still waited for and passed around the trenches in 1914, its popularity was gradually waning. By the end of 1916 it had 'softly and silently vanished away', and when Blatchford died in 1943 he, too, was already half-forgotten.

The *Clarion*'s decline was directly related to Blatchford's inability to understand just how much the British working class had changed over the twenty-five years of its life. Although the paper continually exposed the inequalities of capitalist society, it failed to give any guidance as to how such a society could be changed. As Blatchford was to remark, 'A political Labour paper leaves me cold. It is all the difference between a rose garden and a cabbage patch. I cannot enthuse about cabbages'. And again, 'Convince the people and never mind the parties'.

This attitude inevitably led to a serious underestimation of the political significance of workers' struggles which were taking place both at home and abroad. For instance, in 1910, forty Labour members were elected to Parliament, and only the *Clarion* failed to mention the General Election. Even more important was Blatchford's thinking on the Empire, a vital issue for British workers. His five years in the Army had left its mark. By 1914 his jingoistic tendencies had become all too obvious with his enthusiastic support for the build-up of the British Navy against German competition. The paper's bitter hostility to the Easter rising in Ireland in 1916 reflected just how far Blatchford had moved by that time.

Nevertheless, there can be no doubt about the influence the *Clarion* had, together with **Merrie England**. Although the book's chief weakness lies in its omissions there is much in it which is as relevant today as it was in 1893. It still remains a book for 'the intelligent working-class man and woman', and will continue to do so for many years.

CONTENTS.

MERRIE ENGLAND:

A Series of Letters on the Labour Problem.

ADDRESSED TO JOHN SMITH, OF OLDHAM, A HARD-HEADED WORKMAN, FOND OF FACTS.

By NUNQUAM.

CHAPTER I.

DEAR MR. SMITH,—I am sorry to hear that you look upon the Independent Labour Party as a "Tory dodge," and that you are sometimes pleased to describe me as a "windy crank," and at other times as a "man with an axe to grind."

Nevertheless, as you have good metal in you, and are very numerous, I mean to argue the point with you.

You are a staunch Liberal, and you pride yourself upon being "a shrewd, hard-headed, practical man." You would not pride yourself upon that, for you are naturally over-modest, had you not been told by political orators that you are that kind of man.

Hence you have come to believe that you "entertain a wholesome contempt for theories," and have contracted a habit of calling for "Facts" in a peremptory manner, like a stage brigand calling for "Wine."

Now, Mr. Smith, if you really are a man of hard, shrewd sense, we shall get on very well. I am myself a plain, practical man. I base my beliefs upon what I know and see, and respect "a fact" more than a Lord Mayor.

In these letters I shall stick to the hardest of hard facts, and the coldest of cold reason; and I shall appeal to that robust commonsense and English love of fair-play for which, I understand, you are more famous than for your ability to see beyond the end of your free and independent nose at election times.

I assume, Mr. Smith, that you, as a hard-headed, practical man, would rather be well off than badly off, and that, with regard to your own earnings, you would rather be paid twenty shillings in the pound than four shillings in the pound.

And I assume that, as a humane man, you would rather that others should not suffer, if their suffering can be prevented.

If then, I assert that you are being defrauded, and that others, especially weak women and young children, are enduring much misery and wrong, and if I assert, farther, that I know a means whereby you may obtain justice, and they may secure peace, you will surely, as a kind and sensible man, consent to hear me.

If your roof were leaky, or your business bad, if there were a plague in your city, and all recognised remedies had failed, you would certainly give a hearing to any creditable person who claimed to have found a cure.

I don't mean that you would accept his remedy without examination; that would be foolish, but you would allow him to explain it, and if it seemed reasonable you would try it.

To reject an idea because it is new is not a proof of shrewd sense, it is a proof of bigoted ignorance. Trade unionism was new once, and was denounced by the very same people who now denounce the views I advocate. There were many prominent politicians and writers who declared the railway train and the telegraph to be impossible. There were many who condemned the factory acts. There were many who laughed at the idea of an Atlantic cable, and I remember when it was prophesied of the ballot that it would lead to anarchy and revolution.

To say that an idea is new is not to prove that it is untrue. The oldest idea was new once; and some of my ideas—as, for instance, the idea that justice and health are precious things—are considerably older than the House of Commons or Adam Smith's " Wealth of Nations."

If you wish for an instance of the value of new ideas, Mr. Smith, get a good life of Charles Darwin, and another of George Stephenson, and read them.

I ask you, then, as a practical man, to forget me, and to consider my arguments on their merits.

But I must also ask you to forget yourself. One of the ancients, I think it was Pythagoras, said it was necessary to " get out of the body to think." That means that when a problem is before you you should not let any personal prejudice, or class feeling, come between that problem and your mind—that you should consider a case upon the evidence alone, as a jury should.

Forget, then, that you are a joiner or a spinner, a Catholic or a Freethinker, a Liberal or a Tory, a moderate drinker or a teetotaler, and consider the problem as a *man*.

If you had to do a problem in arithmetic, or if you were cast adrift in an open boat at sea, you would not set to work as a Wesleyan, or a Liberal Unionist; but you would tackle the sum by the rules of arithmetic, and would row the boat by the strength of your own manhood, and keep a look-out for passing ships under *any* flag.

I ask you, then, Mr. Smith, to hear what I have to say, and to decide by your own judgment whether I am right or wrong.

Now then, what is the problem? I call it the problem of life. We have here a Country and a People. The problem is—Given a Country and a People, find how the People may make the best of the Country and of Themselves.

First, then, as to the capacities of the country and the people.

The country is fertile and fruitful, and well stored with nearly all the things that the people need.

The people are intelligent, industrious, strong, and famous for their perseverance, their inventiveness and resource.

It looks, then, as if such a people in such a country must certainly succeed in securing health, and happiness, and plenty for all.

But we know very well that our people, or at least the bulk of them, have neither health, nor pleasure, nor plenty.

These are *facts;* and so far, I assume, you and I are quite in accord.

Now I assert that if the labour of the British people were properly organised and wisely applied, this country would, in return for very little toil, yield abundance for all.

I assert that the labour of the British people is not properly organised, nor wisely applied; and I undertake to show how it might and should be organised and applied, and what would be the results if it were organised and applied in accordance with my suggestions.

The ideal of British Society to-day is the ideal of individual effort, or competition. That is to say, every man for himself. Each citizen is to try as hard as he can to get for himself as much *money* as he can, and to use it for his own pleasure, and leave it for his own children.

That is the present personal ideal. The

present national ideal is to become "The Workshop of the World." That is to say, the British people are to manufacture goods for sale to foreign countries, and in return for those goods are to get more money than they could obtain by developing the resources of their own country for their own use.

My ideal is that each individual should seek his advantage in co-operation with his fellows, and that the people should make the best of their own country before attempting to trade with other peoples.

I propose, Mr. Smith, and I submit the proposal to you, who are a sensible and practical man, as a sensible and practical proposal, that we should first of all ascertain what things are desirable for our health and happiness of body and mind, and that we should then organise our people with the object of producing those things in the best and easiest way.

The idea being to get the best results with the least labour.

And now, Mr. Smith, if you will read the following books for yourself, you will be in a better position to follow me in my future letters :—

Thoreau's "Walden." London: Walter Scott, 1s.
"Problems of Poverty," John Hobson, M.A. London: Methuen, 2s. 6d.
"Industrial History of England," H. de B. Gibbins, M.A. London: Methuen, 2s. 6d.

There are also a Fabian tract called "Facts for Socialists," price one penny, and a pamphlet called "Socialism," a reply to the Pope, price one penny, which will be useful. The last-named pamphlet is by Robert Blatchford, and can be had at the *Clarion* office.

CHAPTER II.

DEAR MR. SMITH,—As I said in my first chapter, the problem we have to consider is :—

Given a country and a people, find how the people may make the best of the country and themselves.

Before we can solve this problem, we must understand the country and the people. We must find out their capacities; that is to say what can be got from the country; what it will yield; and what can be got from ourselves; what we can do and be.

On these points I differ from the so-called practical people of the Manchester School, for I believe that this country will yield a great deal more of the good things of life than the people need ; and that the people can be much happier, healthier, richer, and better than they now are.

But the Manchester School would have us believe that our own country is too barren to feed us, and that our people are too base and foolish to lead pure, wise, and honest lives.

This is a difference as to facts. I will try, presently, to show you that the facts are in my favour.

You, Mr. Smith, are a practical man ; you have reason and judgment. Therefore you would do a pleasant thing in preference to an unpleasant thing. You would choose a healthy and agreeable occupation in preference to an unhealthy and disagreeable occupation. You would rather live in a healthy and agreeable place than in an unhealthy and disagreeable place. You would rather work four hours a day than twelve hours a day. You would rather do the things you like to do, and have the things you wish for, than do the things you dislike to do, and lack the things you wish for.

You live in Oldham, and you are a spinner. If I ask you why you live in Oldham, and why you work in the factory, you will say that you do it in order to "get a living."

I think also that you will agree with me on three points :—Firstly, that Oldham is not a nice place to live in; secondly, that the factory is not a nice place to work in; thirdly, that you don't get as good a living as you desire.

There are some things you do, which you would rather not do ; and there are some things you wish for and cannot get.

Now suppose we try to find out what are the

4 MERRIE ENGLAND.

things it is best for us to have, and which is the best and easiest way to get them.

I hope that up to this point I have been quite clear, and practical, and truthful.

Of course you have read Robinson Crusoe. You know that he was shipwrecked upon an island, and had to provide for himself. He raised corn, tamed goats, dried raisins, built himself a house, and made vessels of clay, clothing of skins, a boat, and other useful things. If he had set to work making bead necklaces and feather fans before he secured food and lodging you would say he was a fool, and that he did not make the most of his time and his island. But what would you call him if he had starved and stinted himself in order to make bead necklaces and feather fans for some other person who was too lazy to work?

Whatever you call him, you may call yourself, for *you* are wasting your time and your chances in the effort to support idle people and vain things.

Now, to our problem. How are we to make the best of our country, and of our lives? What things do we need in order to secure a happy, healthy, and worthy human life?

We may divide the things needful into two kinds: Mental and physical. That is to say, the things needful for the body and the things needful for the mind.

Here again I differ very much from the self-styled practical people of the Manchester School.

My ideal is frugality of body and opulence of mind. I suggest that we should be as temperate and as simple as possible in our use of mere bodily necessaries, so that we may have as much time as possible to enjoy pleasures of a higher, purer, and more delightful kind.

Your Manchester School treat all Social and Industrial problems from the standpoint of mere animal subsistence. They do not seem to think that you *have* any mind. With them it is a question of bread and cheese and be thankful. They are like the man in "Our Mutual Friend" who estimated the needs of the ferryman's daughter in beef and beer. It was a question, he said, "of so many pounds of beef, and so many pints of porter." That beef and that porter were "the fuel to supply that woman's engine," and, of course, she was

only to have just as much fuel as would keep the engine working at high pressure. But I submit to you, Mr. Smith, that such an estimate would be an insult to a horse.

Your Manchester School claim to be practical men, and always swear by facts. As I said before, I reverence facts; but I want *all* the facts; not a few of them. If I am to give a verdict, I must hear the whole of the evidence.

Suppose a gardener imagined that all a flower needed was earth and manure, and so planted his ferns on the sunny side and his peaches on the shady side of his garden. Would you call him a practical man?

You will see what I mean. Soil is a "fact," and manure is a "fact." But the habit of a plant is a "fact" also, and so are sunshine and rain "facts."

Turn, then, from plants to men, and tell me are appetites the only facts of human nature? Do men need nothing but food, and shelter, and clothes?

It is true that bread, and meat, and wages, and sleep are "facts," but they are not the only facts of life. Men have imaginations and passions as well as appetites.

I must ask you, Mr. Smith, to insist upon hearing all the evidence. I must ask you to use your eyes and ears, to examine your memory, to consult your own experience and the experience of the best and wisest men who have lived, and to satisfy yourself that although wheat and cotton and looms and ploughs and bacon and blankets and hunger and thirst and heat and cold are facts, they are not the only facts, nor even the greatest facts of life.

For love is a fact, and hope is a fact, and rest, and laughter, and music, and knowledge are facts; and facts which have to be remembered and have to be reckoned with before we can possibly solve the problem of how the British people are to make the best of their country and themselves.

A life which consists of nothing but eating, and drinking, and sleeping, and working is not a human life—it is the life of a beast. Such a life is not worth living. If we are to spend all our days and nights in a kind of penal servitude, continually toiling and suffering in order to live, we had better break at once the chains of our bitter slavery, and die.

What, then, are the things needful for the body and the mind of man?

The bodily needs are two:—

Health and Sustenance.

The mental needs are three:—

Knowledge,
Pleasure,
Intercourse.

We will consider the bodily needs first, and we will begin by finding out what things ensure good bodily health.

To ensure good health we must lead a "natural" life. The farther we get from nature,—the more artificial our lives become,—the worse is our health.

The chief ends to health are pure air, pure water, pure and sufficient food, cleanliness, exercise, rest, warmth, and ease of mind.

The chief obstacles to health are impure air, impure water, bad or insufficient food, gluttony, drunkenness, vice, dirt, heavy labour, want of rest, exposure, and anxiety of mind.

The sure marks of good health are physical strength and beauty.

Look at a statue of an Ancient Greek Athlete, and then at the form of a Modern Sweater's Slave, and you will see how true this is.

These are facts. Any doctor, or scientist, or artist, or athlete will confirm these statements.

Now I shall show you, later, that hardly any of our people lead natural and healthy lives. I shall show you that the average Briton might be very much healthier, handsomer, and stronger than he is; and I shall show you that the average duration of life might easily be *doubled*.

Next, as to Sustenance. There are four chief things needed to sustain life in a civilised community :—

Food,
Clothing,
Shelter, and
Fuel.

All these things should be used temperately. Enough is *better* than a feast. Luxurious living is a bad and not a good thing. You know that when a man is training for any feat of strength or of endurance he takes plain and pure food, and abundant rest and exercise. A rowing man, a running man, a boxer, a cricketer, or

an athlete of any kind would never think of training on turtle soup, game pies, and champagne. Again I say that any doctor, scientist, artist, or athletic trainer will endorse my statement.

Now I shall show you, later, that our people are badly clothed, and badly fed, and badly housed. That some have more, but most have less, than is good for them; and that with a quarter of the labour now expended in getting improper sustenance we might produce proper sustenance, and plenty of it, for all.

Meanwhile, let us consider the mental needs of life. These are

Knowledge, Pleasure, and Intercourse.

You may describe all these things as pleasures, or as recreations, if you choose.

Of Knowledge there are almost numberless branches, and all of them fascinating. Modern science alone is a vast storehouse of interest and delight. Astronomy, physiology, botany, chemistry, these words sound dry and forbidding to the man who knows nothing at all of the science; but to the student they are more fascinating, more thrilling, and more marvellous than any romance.

But science is only one branch of knowledge. There is literature, there is history, there are foreign countries and peoples, there are languages, and laws, and philosophies to interest and to inform us. Solomon spoke well when he said that wisdom is better than rubies. As a mere *amusement* the acquirement of knowledge is above price. But it has another value, it enables us to help our fellow creatures, and to leave the world better than we found it.

As for Pleasures their name is legion. There are such pleasures as walking, rowing, swimming, football, cricket. There are the arts, and the drama. There are the beauties of nature. There are travel and adventure. Mere words cannot convey an idea of the intensity of these pleasures. Music alone is more delightful and more precious than all the vanities wealth can buy, or all the carnal luxuries that folly can desire. The varieties of pure and healthy pleasures are infinite.

Then as to Intercourse. I mean by that all the exaltation and all the happiness that we can get from friendship, from love, from comradeship, and from family ties. These are amongst the best and the sweetest things that life can give.

Now, Mr. Smith, you are a practical and a sensible man. I ask you to look about you and to think, and then to tell me what share of all these things falls to the share of the bulk of the British people ; but especially to the share of the great working masses.

In the average lot of the average British workman how much knowledge and culture, and science and art, and music and the drama, and literature and poetry, and field sports and exercise, and travel and change of scene ?

You know very well that our working people get little of these things, and you know that such as they get are of inferior quality.

Now I say to you that the people do not get enough of the things needful for body and mind, that they do not get them of the best, and that they do not get them because they have neither money to pay for them nor leisure to enjoy them.

I say, farther, that they ought to have and might have abundance of these things, and I undertake to show you how they can obtain them.

We hear a great deal, Mr. Smith, about the " Struggle for Existence."

Well, I say there is no need for any " struggle for existence." I have shown you what things are necessary to a happy and noble existence, and I say to you now that all these things can be easily and abundantly produced.

Given our country and our people I maintain that the people, if rightly organised and directed, can get from the country *all* that is good for them, with very little labour.

The work needed to supply the bodily and mental needs above enumerated is very slight. The best things of life—knowledge, art, recreation, friendship, and love—are all *cheap;* that is to say they can all be got with little labour.

Why then the " struggle for existence " ?

So far, Mr. Smith, I have, I hope, been practical and plain. I have indulged in no fine writing, I have used no hard words, I have kept close to facts. There has been nothing " windy " or " sentimental " up to now. I shall be still more practical as we go on.

In the meantime, if you can find Ruskin's Modern Painters in your free library, I should advise you to read it.

CHAPTER III.

DEAR MR. SMITH,—Before we begin this chapter I must ask you to keep in mind the fact that a man's bodily wants are few.

I shall be well outside the mark if I say that a full grown healthy man can be well fed upon a daily ration of

1 lb. of bread,
1 lb. of vegetables,
1 lb. of meat.

Add to this a few groceries, a little fruit, some luxuries, in the shape of wine, beer, and tobacco ; a shelter, a bed, some clothing, and a few tools and articles of furniture, and you have all the material things you need.

Remember, also, that when you have got these things you have got all the material things you can use. A millionaire or a

monarch could hardly use more, or if he did use more would use them to his hurt and not to his advantage.

You, Mr. Smith, live in Oldham and work in the factory in order to get a living. " A living" consists of the things above mentioned.

I ask you, as a practical, sensible man, whether it is not possible to get those few simple things with less labour ; and whether it is not possible to add to them health and the leisure to enjoy life and develop the mind?

The Manchester School will tell you that you are very fortunate to get as much as you do, and that he is a dreamer or a knave who persuades you that you can get more.

The Manchester School is the Commercial School. The supporters of that school will tell you that you cannot prosper, that is to say you cannot "get a living," without the capitalist, without open competition, and without a great foreign trade.

They will tell you that you would be very foolish to raise your own food stuffs here in England so long as you can buy them more cheaply from foreign nations. They will tell you that this country is incapable of producing enough food for her present population, and that therefore your very existence depends upon keeping the foreign trade in your hands.

Now, I shall try to prove to you that every one of these statements is untrue. I shall try to satisfy you that :—

    1. The capitalist is a curse, and not a blessing.
    2. That competition is wasteful, and cruel, and wrong.
    3. That no foreign country can sell us food more cheaply than we can produce it; and
    4. That this country is capable of feeding more than treble her present population.

We hear a lot about the greatness and the glory of our foreign trade, and are always being reminded how much we owe to our factory system, and how proud of it we ought to be.

I hate the factory system, I despise the factory system, and I denounce the factory system as a hideous, brutal, futile, and false thing. This is one of the reasons why the Manchester School call me a dreamer and a dangerous agitator. I will state my case to you plainly, and ask you for a verdict in accordance with the evidence.

My reasons for attacking the factory system are :—

    1. Because it is ugly, disagreeable, and mechanical.
    2. Because it is injurious to public health.
    3. Because it is unnecessary.
    4. Because it is a danger to the national existence.

The Manchester School will tell you that the destiny of this country is to become "The Workshop of the World."

I say that is not true ; and that it would be a thing to deplore if it were true. The idea that this country is to be the "Workshop of the World" is a wilder dream than any that

the wildest Socialist ever cherished. But if this country did become the "Workshop of the World" it would at the same time become the most horrible and the most miserable country the world has ever known.

Now, Mr. Smith, let us be practical, and look at the facts.

First, as to the question of beauty and pleasantness. You know the factory districts of Lancashire. I ask you is it not true that they are ugly, and dirty, and smoky, and disagreeable ? Compare the busy towns of Lancashire of Staffordshire, of Durham, and of South Wales, with the country towns of Surrey, Suffolk, and Hants.

In the latter counties you will get pure air, bright skies, clear rivers, clean streets, and beautiful fields, woods, and gardens ; you will get cattle and streams, and birds and flowers, and you know that all these things are well worth having, and that none of them can exist side by side with the factory system.

I know that the Manchester School will tell you that this is "mere sentiment." But compare their actions with their words.

Do you find the champions of the factory system despising nature, and beauty, and art, and health—except in their speeches and lectures to you ?

No. You will find these people living as far from the factories as they can get ; and you will find them spending their long holidays in the most beautiful parts of England, Scotland, Ireland, or the Continent.

The pleasures they enjoy are denied to you. They preach the advantages of the factory system because they reap the benefits while you bear the evils.

To make wealth for themselves they destroy the beauty and the health of your dwelling places ; and then they sit in their suburban villas, or on the hills and terraces of the lovely southern countries, and sneer at the "sentimentality" of the men who ask you to cherish beauty and to prize health.

Or they point out to you the value of the "wages" which the factory system brings you, reminding you that you have carpets on your floors, and pianos in 'your parlours, and a week's holiday at Blackpool once a year.

But how much health or pleasure can you

get out of a cheap and vulgar carpet? And
what is the use of a piano if you have neither
leisure nor means to learn to play it? And
why should you prize that one week in the
crowded, noisy watering-place, if health and
fresh air and the great salt sea are mere
sentimental follies?

And let me ask you is any carpet so beauti-

sake of being able once a year to go to
Blackpool, and once a night to listen to a
cracked piano?

Now I tell you, my practical friend, that you
ought to have, and may have, good music, and
good homes, and a fair and healthy country,
and more of all the things that make life
sweet; that you may have them at less cost

MAP 1.

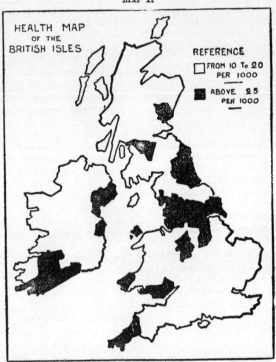

HEALTH MAP
OF THE
BRITISH ISLES

REFERENCE

☐ FROM 10 To 20
   PER 1000

■ ABOVE 25
   PER 1000

ful or so pleasant as a carpet of grass and
daisies? Is the fifth-rate music you play
upon your cheap pianos as sweet as the songs
of the gushing streams and joyous birds? And
does a week at a spoiled and vulgar watering-
place repay you for fifty-one weeks' toil and
smother in a hideous and stinking town?

As a practical man, would you of your own
choice convert a healthy and beautiful country
like Surrey into an unhealthy and hideous
country like Wigan or Cradley, just for the

of labour than you now pay for the privilege
of existing in Oldham; and that you can *never*
have them if England becomes " the Workshop
of the World."

But the relative beauty and pleasantness
of the factory and country districts do not
need demonstration. The ugliness of Widnes
and Sheffield and the beauty of Dorking and
Monsal Dale are not matters of sentiment
nor of argument—they are matters of fact.
The value of beauty is not a matter of senti-

ment: it is a fact. You would rather see a squirrel than a sewer rat. You would rather bathe in the Avon than in the Irwell. You would prefer the fragrance of a rose-garden to the stench of a sewage works. You would prefer Bolton Woods to Ancoats slums.

As for those who sneer at beauty, as they spend fortunes on pictures, on architecture

Pure air, pure water, pure and sufficient food, cleanliness, exercise, rest, warmth, and ease of mind.

What are the invariable accompaniments of the factory system?

Foul air, foul water, adulterated foods, dirt, long hours of sedentary labour and continual anxiety as to wages and employment in the

MAP 2.

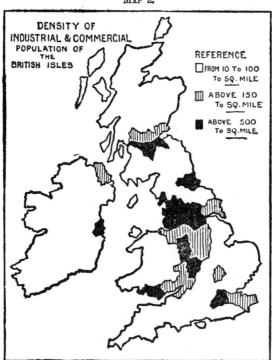

DENSITY OF
INDUSTRIAL & COMMERCIAL
POPULATION OF
THE
BRITISH ISLES

REFERENCE
☐ FROM 10 To 100
To SQ. MILE

▥ ABOVE 150
To SQ. MILE

■ ABOVE 500
To SQ. MILE

and on foreign tours, they put themselves out of court.

Sentiment or no sentiment, Mr. Smith, beauty is better than ugliness, and health is better than disease, and the man who denies this is either a rogue or a fool.

Now under the factory system you must sacrifice both health and beauty.

As to my second objection—the evil effect of the factory system on the public health. What are the chief means to health?

present, added to a terrible uncertainty as to existence in the future.

Look through any great industrial town, in the colliery, the iron, the silk, the cotton, or the woollen industries, and you will find hard work, unhealthy work, vile air, overcrowding, disease, ugliness, drunkenness, and a high death-rate. These are *facts*.

To begin with I give you outline maps, copied from Bartholomew's Gazetteer of the British Islands, which is the best work of its class extant.

10 MERRIE ENGLAND.

Map 1 shows the death-rates in the British Isles.

Map 2 shows the distribution of manufactures in the British Isles.

Now examine these maps and you will find that where the manufactures are the greatest the death-rate is the highest, and the population the most dense.

Turn from Bartholomew's Gazetteer to the Registrar - General's returns. The average death-rate for England and Wales from 1881 to 1890 was 19·1 in the thousand. The death-rate of Lancashire for the same period was 22·5 per thousand. But to get a fair idea of the difference between town and country we must contrast Lancashire with the agricultural counties. Here are eight county death-rates from 1881 to 1890:—

Surrey	16·1
Kent	16·6
Sussex	15·7
Hants	16·8
Berks	16·2
Wilts	16·9
Dorset	16·2
Lancashire	22·5

In 1887, the latest year for which I have the figures, the death-rates in some of the principal Lancashire towns were:—

Bolton	21·31
Oldham	23·84
Salford	23·95
Preston	27·0
Blackburn	25·48
Manchester	28·67

And in that year the average death-rate in Surrey and Sussex was 16·3.

Now observe the difference between Lancashire and Surrey. It is a difference of 6 to the thousand. Lancashire in 1881 contained 3½ millions of people, or 3,500 thousands, so that the excess of deaths in the cotton county reaches the total of 21,000.

But again, in the Registrar-General's returns for 1891 I find two tables showing the annual deaths per 100,000 of children under one year, for 1889, 1890, 1891. The first table shows the figures for the three counties of Hertford, Wilts, and Dorset; the second for the three towns, Preston, Leicester, and Blackburn.

Three farming counties	9,717
Three manufacturing towns	21,803

That is to say that the death-rate of children in those three towns is more than twice as high as the death-rate of children in those three counties.

But, again, Dr. Marshall, giving statistics of recruiting in this country, shows that not only were the country recruits taller than those from the towns, but he adds that "in every case the men born in the country were found to have better chests than those born in towns, the difference in chest measurement being proportionately greater than the difference in stature." According to Dr. Beddoe:—

The natives of Edinburgh and Glasgow are on an average from one to two inches shorter, and about fifteen to twenty pounds lighter, than the rural population of various parts of Scotland. The statistics of the Northumberland Light Infantry give 5ft. 6in. as the height of the natives of Newcastle; while the rural volunteers have an average height of from 5ft. 8in. to 5ft. 10in., and are "of course much heavier than the townsmen."

Drs. Chassagne and Dally, in a work on gymnasia, give tables comparing the rustics and townsmen of France, which show the former to be taller and more robust. Indeed, as Mr. Gattie, in an article on the physique of European armies, says:—

A glance at the tables suffices to show the physical superiority of the countrymen at all points. Looking more closely, we find that, although the townsmen who had followed outdoor pursuits were shorter and lighter than the rest, they were able to lift and carry much greater weights.

Again, the official statistics of Switzerland tell the same story, thus:—

The butchers and bakers have much the best development, both of arm and chest; the carpenters, blacksmiths, and masons coming next. The bakers are not so tall as the butchers, blacksmiths, and carpenters, and the masons are very much shorter, but their arms are proportionately better developed than those of the carpenters and blacksmiths. The agricultural labourers and cheesemen are next in order, and then follow the wheelwrights, saddlers, and sedentary operatives, *the weakest men of all being the weavers*; while the tailors are the shortest, and are scarcely less feeble.

These, Mr. Smith, are facts; and they seem to prove my second point, that the factory system is bad for the public health.

CHAPTER IV.

DEAR MR. SMITH,—We come now to the third objection to the factory system—that it is unnecessary. It is often asserted that this country could not feed all her present population. I will try to show you that this is absurd. But first of all let me recommend to you Sketchley's "Review of European Society," price 1s. 6d. (William Reeves, London); and "Poverty and the State," by Herbert V. Mills (Kegan Paul, Trench, and Co.).

We have to prove that the British Islands can grow wheat enough to feed 36 millions of people.

In Hoyle's "Sources of Wealth" it is stated that England and Wales contain about 50 millions of acres of good land, unbuilt upon and available for agriculture.

Lord Lauderdale estimates that 500 acres will feed 2,000 people, that is four to the acre. Therefore if we used *all* our available land we could feed 200 millions of people.

Take a lower estimate. Allison estimates, in his "Principles of Population," that, after allowing for bad land and pasture land, these islands could feed the following numbers:—

England and Wales	60,000,000
Scotland	15,000,000
Ireland	48,000,000
Total	123,000,000

But these are estimates. Take accomplished facts. The *Quarterly Review* said in 1873 that in the year 1841 England grew wheat at home for 24 millions of people.

Now read this quotation, from a speech of Mr. Cobden's at Manchester:—

I have heard Mr. Oglivey say—and he is willing to go before a committee of the House to prove it—that Cheshire, if properly cultivated, is capable of producing three times as much as it now produces from its surface . . . and there is not a higher authority in the kingdom.

That was in 1844, at a time when England grew wheat for 24,000,000 of its people.

The Manchester School would have us believe that we cannot feed 36 millions. Well, in 1885 we imported nearly £53,000,000 worth of foreign wheat.

Compare that sum with the following statement by Mr. Mechi:—

I have tested this by comparative results, and find that if all the land in this kingdom equal to my own, about 50 million acres, produced as much per acre as mine does, our agricultural produce would be increased by the enormous amount of £421,000,000 annually.

So much for the possible yield of our land under ordinary cultivation.

But now comes the most tremendous idea—the idea of what is called "intensive agriculture."

In an article in the *Forum* in 1890, Prince Krapotkin says that when we learn how to use the soil we may feed ten times our population with ease. This, he says, has been proved in France. Note this:—

That, by combining a series of such simple operations as the selections of seeds, sowing in rows, and proper manuring, the crops can be increased by at least 75 per cent. over the best present average, while the cost of production can be reduced by 50 per cent. by the use of some inexpensive machinery, to say nothing of costly machines, like the steam digger, or the pulverisers which make the soil required for each special culture.

The Prince is right. Agriculture has been neglected because all the mechanical and chemical skill, and all the capital and energy of man, have been thrown into the struggle for trade profits and manufacturing pre-eminence. We want a few Farradays, Watts, Stephensons, and Cobdens to devote their genius and industry to the great food question. Once let the public interest and the public genius be concentrated upon the agriculture of England, and we shall soon get silenced the croakers who talk about the impossibility of the country feeding her people.

But, again, Prince Krapotkin says:—

Mr. Hallett, by a simple selection of grains, will obtain in a few years a wheat which bears 10,840 grains on each stem grown from a single seed; so that from seven to eight hundred of his stems of wheat (which could be grown upon a score of square yards) would give the yearly supply of bread for a full-grown person.

Twenty square yards to feed one person. Then one acre would feed 242 persons; so that to find bread for our entire population of 36 millions we need only 148,763 acres.

When I add that Devonshire contains 1,665,208 acres, that Surrey contains 485,129 acres, and Kent 995,392 acres, I think you will see that we need not depend upon America for our wheat.

Nor is that all. The *Review of Reviews*, in its notice on this valuable paper of Prince Krapotkin's, says :—

Prince Krapotkin's chief illustrations, however, as to the possibility of intensive agriculture are taken from the Channel Islands, and notably from Guernsey. Guernsey has 1,300 persons to the square mile, and has more unproductive soil than Jersey ; but Guernsey leads the world in the matter of advanced agriculture, because Guernsey is being practically roofed in. The Guernsey kitchen garden is all under glass. Prince Krapotkin found in one place three-fourths of an acre covered with glass ; in another, in Jersey, he found vineries under glass covering thirteen acres, and yielding more money return than that which can be taken from an ordinary English farm of 1,300 acres. Each acre of greenhouse employs three men. The cost of erecting them is about ten shillings per square yard, excluding the cost of the heating pipes. The thirteen acres are warmed by consuming a thousand cart loads of coke and coal. Prince Krapotkin sees before long that immense vineries will grow up round the coal pits of Northumberland, where artificial heat can be obtained from coals selling at the cost of three shillings the ton.

Depend upon it, what I have told you is true, and that England can feed her people as she has fed them in times gone by, with never a factory flue to vomit foulness into the air, and never a greedy money-grasper to poison her streams with filth, or wither her woods and glades with soot and sulphur.

We will next proceed to consider my fourth objection to the factory system, when I think I shall be able to show you, beyond all question, that besides being hideous, unpleasant, unhealthy, and unnecessary, the factories are a serious danger to the existence of the Empire.

Granting that the factory system is an evil, is it a necessary evil ?

Why do we weave cloth and cotton ? For two purposes :—

1. To clothe ourselves.
2. To exchange for foreign produce.

To provide for our own needs we must make cotton or linen fabrics. True. But we need not make them by steam power. We could make them by water power, and so abolish the smoke nuisance.

Will you have the goodness, Mr. Smith, to cast your eyes over the following statements, made, a few years ago, by Prof. Thompson :—

The average rise and fall of the tide at the city of Bristol, five miles from its mouth, is 23 feet. According to calculations I have made from the average volume of water displaced up and down each tide, there are no fewer than 20 billions foot-pounds of energy wasted each year, or enough to charge 10 million Faure cells. At the mouth of the river the total annual energy thus running to utter waste cannot be less than 50 billions foot-pounds, and in the rapid currents of the river Severn, with their enormous tides of great volume, the tidal energy must be practically unlimited. A tenth part of the tidal energy in the gorge of the Avon would light the city of Bristol ; a tenth part of the tidal energy in the channel of the Severn would light every city ; and another tenth part would turn every loom and spindle and axle in Great Britain.

The power of water is tremendous ; the beauty of water is sublime. Perhaps, when our practical men learn a little common sense, we shall be able to grind an axe or throw a shuttle without blackening the sky above or choking the unhappy creatures who crawl upon the earth beneath. Besides, the less coal needed, the fewer colliers needed, and in the *Clarion* Tito has told us that ninety thousand men and boys are killed and injured every year in the mines.

Now, Mr. Smith, why should we make cotton goods for foreign countries ?

The Manchester School will tell you that we must do it to buy corn. In 1885 we exported cotton goods to the value of £66,000,000 ; and we imported corn and flour, in the same year, to the value of £53,000,000.

Why? The Manchester School will tell you that we cannot grow our own corn. That is not true.

They will tell you that as foreigners can grow corn more cheaply than we can, and as we can make cotton goods more cheaply than they can, it is to the interest of both parties to exchange.

I do not believe that any nation can sell corn more cheaply than we *could* produce it ; and I am sure that even if it cost a little more to grow our own corn than to buy it, yet it would be to our interest to grow it. First as to the cost of growing corn. In the Industrial History of England I find the question of why the English farmer is undersold answered in this way:—

The answer is simple. His capital has been filched from him, surely, but not always slowly, by a tremendous increase in his rent. The landlords of the eighteenth century made the English farmer the foremost agriculturalist in the world, but their successors of the nineteenth have ruined him by their extortions. . . . In 1799 we find land paying nearly 20s. an acre. . . . By 1850 it had risen to 38s. 6d. . . . £2 an acre was not an uncommon rent for land a few years ago, the average increase of English rent being no less than 26½ per cent. between 1854 and 1879. . . . The result has been that the average capital per acre now employed in agriculture is only about £4 or £5, instead of at least £10, as it ought to be.

I know it has been said, and is said, that an English farmer owning his land cannot compete with foreign dealers; but I think that is doubtful, and I am sure that if the land were owned by the State, and farmed systematically by the best methods, we might grow our corn more cheaply than we could buy it.

But suppose we could not. The logical result of the free-trade argument would be that British agriculture must perish. The case was very clearly put by Mr. Cobden in the House of Commons:—

To buy in the cheapest market and sell in the dearest, what is the meaning of the maxim? It means that you take the article which you have in the greatest abundance, and with it obtain from others that of which they have the most to spare; so giving to mankind the means of enjoying the fullest abundance of earth's goods.

Yes, it means that, but it means much more than that. However, let us reduce these fine phrases to figures. Suppose America can send us wheat at 30s. a quarter; and suppose ours cost 35s. a quarter, which is giving the Manchester men a big margin, then, as we import fifty-three million pounds' worth of corn each year, that means a saving of seven-and-a-half millions a year. The rent paid for land and buildings in this country is stated at two hundred millions. *The whole of that is wasted.*

But now, even if we gain seven-and-a-half million pounds by buying foreign wheat, there remains the question, *do we lose nothing?* The gain is ⅐ in the cost of wheat, *we get a loaf for 3d. instead of having to pay 3¼d. That is all the fine phrases mean.*

What do we lose? We lose the beauty and health of our factory towns; we lose annually some twenty thousand lives in Lancashire alone; we are in constant danger of great strikes, like that which recently so crushed our cotton-operatives; we are reduced to the meanest shifts and the most violent acts of piracy and slaughter to "open up markets" for our goods; we lose the stamina of our people; and—*we lose our agriculture.*

Did you ever consider what it involves, this ruin of British agriculture? Do you know how rapidly the ruin is being wrought? Here is a list, from the *Quarterly Review*, of 1873, of the relative proportions of home-grown and foreign-grown wheat used in this country:—

	Population dependent on home-grown wheat.	Population dependent on foreign wheat.
1821	18,800,000	600,000
1831	21,850,000	700,000
1841	24,280,000	1,200,000
1851	24,550,000	3,930,000
1861	21,500,000	6,706,000
1871	19,278,000	11,661,000

And to this Mr. Sketchley adds his estimate for 1880, which is:—

	Home-grown wheat.	Foreign wheat.
1880	12,152,000	22,352,000

Now, suppose we get at last to a state of things under which thirty-six millions live on foreign-grown wheat and none on wheat of home growth! Suppose our agriculture is dead; and we depend entirely upon foreigners for our daily bread! What will be our position then?

Our position will be this. We shall be unable to produce our own food, and can only get it by selling to foreign countries our manufactured goods. We must buy wheat from America with cotton goods; but first of all we must buy raw cotton with which to make those goods.

We are therefore entirely dependent upon foreigners for our *existence.*

Very well. Suppose we go to war with America! What happens? Do you remember the cotton famine? That was bad; but a mere trifle to what an Anglo-American war would be. We should, in fact, be beaten without firing a shot. America need only close her ports to corn and cotton and we should be starved into surrender, and acceptance of her terms.

Or suppose a European war; say with France, or Russia. *All* our goods and *all* our food has to be brought over sea. What would it cost us to keep command of the seas? What would the effect of the panic be here? And suppose we found our communications cut. We should be starved into surrender at once.

Or suppose France at war with America. Our sufferings would be something terrible.

Tory orators and Jingo poets are fond of shouting of the glories of the Empire and the safety of our possessions ; and reams of paper have been covered with patriotic songs about our "silver streak" and our "tight little island." But don't you see, Mr. Smith, that if we lose our power to feed ourselves *we destroy the advantages of our insular position?* Don't you see that if we destroy our agriculture we destroy our independence at a blow, and become a defenceless nation? Don't you see that the people who depend on foreigners for their food are at the mercy of any ambitious statesman who chooses to make war upon them? And don't you think that is a rather stiff price to pay to get a farthing off the loaf?

Well, Mr. Smith, thanks to the Manchester School, to the factory system, and to the grasping landlord—who is generally a Tory and fond of barging about the security of the Empire—we are almost helpless *now*. Another twenty years of prosperous trade and cheap bread, and we are done for.

Again, how shall we look if, after we have killed our agriculture, we lose our trade? Do you think that impossible? Your cotton-lords seem to think it possible enough, and are now telling you that the only means of keeping the trade which is to kill your agriculture and destroy your national independence is to *lower your wages.*

That farthing off the loaf is going to cost you dear, John Smith, before you have done with it.

Your trade union leaders tell you that you have beaten all foreign competition *except that of India.*

Do you think that you can fight India, John? I don't. Because in India labour is so cheap, and because your cotton-lords, John, some of whom are Liberals, and friends of the people, John, and others of whom are Tories,

who would die for the safety of the Empire, John, will take precious good care to use that cheap Indian labour to bring down your wages, John, by means of competition. Oh, John, John, you silly fellow, have you no eyes?

Well, these are some of the reasons why I don't love the factory system, Mr. Smith. Consider them ; and read the history of that system, and how its first successes were bought by the murder and torture of little children, and spent in buying the freedom of West Indian slaves and in waging war against the French Republic.

The thing is accursed, John. It is cursed in its origin, in its progress, in its methods, in its motives, and in its effects. No nation can be sound whose motive power is greed. No nation can be secure unless it is independent, no nation can be independent unless it is based upon agriculture.

Will you consider this passage from "Field and Hedgerow," by Richard Jefferies, a beautiful book, and well worth buying :—

Of the broad surface of the golden wheat and its glory I have already spoken, yet these flower-encircled acres, these beautiful fields of peaceful wheat, are the battle-fields of life. . . . The wheat-fields are the battle-fields of the world. If not so openly invaded as of old time, the struggle between nations is still one for the ownership or for the control of corn. When Italy became a vineyard and could no more feed armies, slowly power slipped away, and the great empire of Rome split into many pieces. It has long been foreseen that if ever England is occupied with a great war, the question of our corn supply, so largely derived from abroad, will become a weighty matter. . . .

As persons, each of us, in our voluntary and involuntary struggle for money, is really striving for those little grains of wheat that lie so lightly in the palm of the hand. Corn is coin, and coin is corn, and whether it be a labourer in the field, who no sooner receives his weekly wage than he exchanges it for bread, or whether it be the financier in Lombard-street who loans millions, the object is really the same—wheat.

All ends in the same: iron mines, coal mines, factories, furnaces, the counter, the desk—no one can live on iron, or coal, or cotton—the object is really sacks of wheat.

Now, John, is that good sense? Is it nothing to you, John, that the Tory land-grabber and the Liberal money-grubber are killing the wheat fields of England?

Oh, John, and *you* call yourself a practical man. And you don't even know that men live by bread, and think me a fool when I tell you so.

CHAPTER V.

THE problem of life, Mr. Smith, is, "Given a country and a people, show how the people can make the most of the country and themselves." Before we go on, let us try to judge how far we in Britain have succeeded in answering the problem.

The following are facts which no man attempts to deny:—

1. Large numbers of honest and industrious people are badly fed, badly clothed, and badly housed.

2. Many thousands of people die every year from preventable diseases.

3. The average duration of life amongst the population is unnaturally short.

4. Very many people, after lives of toil, are obliged to seek refuge in the workhouse, where they die despised and neglected, branded with the shameful brand of pauperism.

5. It is an almost invariable rule that those who work hardest and longest in this country are the worst paid and the least respected.

6. The wealthiest men in our nation are men who never did a useful day's work.

7. Wealth and power are more prized and more honoured than wisdom, or industry, or virtue.

8. Hundreds of thousands of men and women, willing to work, are unable to find employment.

9. While on the one hand wages are lowered on account of over-production of coal, of cotton, and of corn, on the other hand many of our working people are short of bread, of fuel, and of clothing.

10. Nearly all the land and property in this country are owned by a few idlers, and most of the laws are made in the interests of those few rich people.

11. The national agriculture is going rapidly to ruin to the great injury and peril of the State.

12. Through competition millions of men are employed in useless and undignified work, and all the industrial machinery of the nation is thrown out of gear, so that one greedy rascal may overreach another.

And we are told, Mr. Smith, that all these things must remain as they are, in order that you may be able to "get a living."

What sort of a living do you get?

Your life may be divided into four sections: Working, eating, recreation, and sleeping.

As to work. You are employed in a factory for from 55 to 70 hours a week. Some of your comrades work harder, and longer, and in worse places. Still, as a rule, it may be said of all your class that the hours of labour are too long, that the labour is monotonous, mechanical, and severe, and that the surroundings are often unhealthy, nearly always disagreeable, and in many cases dangerous.

Do you know the difference, Mr. Smith, between "work" and "toil"? It is the difference between the work of the gardener and the toil of the navvy—between the work of the wood carver and the toil of the wood chopper.

We hear a good deal of talk about the idleness of the labouring classes and the industry of the professional classes. There is a difference in the *work*. The surgeon, or the sculptor, following the work of his *choice*, may well work harder than the collier, drudging for a daily wage.

An artist loves his work, and sees in it the means of winning fame, perhaps fortune; an artisan sees in his toil a dull mechanical task, to be done for bread, but never to be made to yield pleasure, or praise, or profit.

As a rule, Mr. Smith, your work is hard and disagreeable.

Now, what are your wages?

I don't mean how many shillings a week do you get; but what *life* do you get as the reward of your toil?

You may get fifteen shillings a week, or a pound, or twenty-five or thirty-five shillings, or two pounds; but the question is how do you *live*? What will your money *buy*?

As I have shown already, you do not get enough leisure, nor enough fresh air, nor enough education, nor enough health, and your town is very ugly and very dirty and very dull. But let us go into details.

I have often seen you, Mr. Smith, turn up your nose with scorn at the sight of a gipsy. Yet the gipsy is a healthier, a stronger, a braver and a wiser man than you, and lives a life more pleasant and free and natural than yours.

Not that the gipsy is a model citizen; but you may learn a great deal from him; and I doubt whether there is anything he could learn from you.

And now let us see how you live. First of all, in the matter of food. Your diet is not a good one. It is not varied enough, and nearly all the things you eat and drink are adulterated.

I am much inclined to think that a vegetarian diet is the best, and I am sure that alcoholic liquors are unnecessary. But this by the way. If you *do* drink beer and spirits it would be better to have them pure. At present nearly all your liquors are abominable.

But there is one thing about your diet worse even than the quality of the food, and that is the cookery. Mrs. Smith is an excellent woman, and I hereby make my bow to her, but she does not know what cookery means.

John Smith, it is a solemn and an awful truth, one which it pains me to utter, but you never ate a beef steak, and you never saw a cooked potato.

God strengthen thy digestion, John, 'tis sore tried. Oh, the soddened vegetables, the flabby fish, the leathery steak, and juiceless joint, I know them, John. Alas! Cookery is an *art*, John, and almost a lost art in this country; or shall we say, an art unfound?

Poor Mrs. Smith gets married and faces the paste-board and the oven with the courage of desperation, and the hope of ignorance. She resembles the young man who had never played the fiddle, but had no doubt he could play it if he tried. And sometimes he *does* try, and so Mrs. Smith tries to cook.

From food we will turn to clothing. Oh, John, John Smith, it is pitiful. Do you know the meaning of the words "form" and "colour"? Look at our people's dress. Observe the cut of it, the general drabness, grayness, and gloom. Those awful black bugles, John, those horrific sack coats, those deadly hats and bonnets, and they do say, John, that crinoline— Ah, heaven! That we should call these delicate creatures ours and not their fashion plates. John, the dresses, but especially the Sunday clothes, of the British working-classes are things too sad for tears.

Costume, John, should be simple, healthy, convenient, and beautiful. Modern British costume is none of these.

This is chiefly because the fashion of our dress is left to fops and tailors, whereas it ought to be left to artists and designers.

But besides the ugliness of your dress, John, it is also true that it is *mean*. It is mean because hardly anything you wear is what it pretends to be, because it is adulterated and jerry-made, and because it is insufficient. Yes, John, in nearly all your houses there is, despite our factory system, a decided scarcity of shirts and socks and sheets and towels and table linen.

Come we now to the home. Your houses, John, are not what they should be. I do not allude to the inferior cottage—*that* is beneath notice. Here in Manchester we have some forty thousand houses unfit for habitation. But let us consider the abode of the more fortunate artisan. It has many faults. It is badly built, badly arranged, and badly fitted. The sanitation is bad. The rooms are much too small. There are no proper appliances for cleanliness. The windows are not big enough. There is a painful dearth of light and air. The cooking appliances are simply barbarous.

Again, the houses are very ugly and *mean*. The streets are too narrow. There are no gardens. There are no trees. Few working-class families have enough bedrooms, and the bathroom is a luxury not known in cottages.

In fine, your houses are ugly, unhealthy, inconvenient, dark, ill-built, ill-fitted, and dear.

This is due, in a great measure, to the cost of land. I will tell you soon why land is so expensive.

Moreover, Mr. Smith, instead of your making the most of your room you will persist in crowding your house with hideous and unnecessary furniture. Furniture, John, is one of your household gods. You are a victim to your furniture, and your wife is a slave. Did it ever occur to you, Mr. Smith, that your only use for the bulk of your household goods is to clean them? It is so, and yet you keep on striving to get more and more furniture for your wife to wait upon.

Just cast your eye over the following description of a Japanese house, John, and see if it does not suggest something to you; and *do* read " Walden." It is only a shilling, and if you read it well it will save you much money in furniture, and your wife much toil in acting as a slave to the sideboard and best parlour suite :—

Simplicity and refinement are the essential characteristics of life in Japan, observes the *Hospital*. The houses, which are spacious, are constructed without foundations. Light wooden uprights resting on flat stones support the thatched or tiled roof. The walls, both outside and those which divide the rooms, are formed of latticed panels which slide over one another, or can be removed altogether if desired. These panels are filled with translucent paper. At night the house is closed in with wooden shutters. The rooms, which are raised about a foot above the ground, are covered with soft padded matting kept spotlessly clean. In the centre of the living room is a shallow square pit lined with metal and filled with charcoal, for the purposes of cooking and warming, or the rooms are warmed with movable metal braziers. *There is no furniture present, no chairs, tables, beds, chests of drawers, pictures, or knick-knacks.* The matted floor serves alike for chairs, table, and bed. To keep it absolutely clean all boots, shoes, and sandals are left on the ground outside. The absence of furniture means the absence of many cares, and as two wooden chopsticks and small lacquer bowls serve for all the purposes of eating, there is no need for plate, glass, knives, forks, spoons, dinner services, and table linen. Thus life is simplified, though it loses at the same time none of its refinement, for *no people can be more dainty and particular in their food, more neat and beautiful in dress*, and more courteous and self-restrained in manner than the Japanese. Kneeling on the floor all work is done, and at night time the padded quilts or futons are spread on the matting, and, with one quilt beneath and another above, sleep can be enjoyed as comfortably as in bed. Before the evening meal is taken it is the invariable custom throughout Japan for every member of the household to take a dip in the family bath, which is heated to a temperature of 110 deg. to 120 deg., at which heat it is found to be very refreshing.

Now, John, if you have any respect and love for your wife you will not need to be told that her lot is a hard one.

Poor Mrs. John Smith, her life is one long slavery. Cooking, cleaning, managing, mending, washing clothes, waiting on husband and children, her work is never done. And amid it all she suffers the pains and anxieties of child-bearing, and the suckling of children.

There are no servants, and few workers, so hard wrought and so ill-paid as the wife of a British artisan. What are her *hours of labour*, my trade union friend? What pleasure has she, what rest, what prospect ?

Cannot be helped, do you say? Nonsense. Do you suppose the Japanese wife works as your wife works ? Not at all. My dear John, in your domestic as in your industrial and political affairs, all that is needed is a little common sense. We are living at present in a state of anarchy and barbarism, and it is *your* fault, and not the fault of the priests and politicians who dupe and plunder you.

And now we come to the last item in your life, your recreation. Here, Mr. Smith, you are very badly served. You have hardly anything to amuse you. Music, art, athletics, science, the drama, and nature are almost denied to you. A few cheerless museums filled with Indian war clubs, fag ends of tapestry, and dried beetles ; a few third-rate pictures, a theatre or two where you have choice between vulgar burlesque and morbid melodrama, a sprinkling of wretched music (?) halls, one or two sleepy night-schools, a football field and sometimes—for the better paid workers—a cricket ground, make up the sum of your life's pleasures. Well—yes, there are plenty of public-houses, and you can gamble. The betting lists and racing news have a corner in all the respectable papers.

One of the most palpable and painful deficiences, John, in all your towns is the deficiency of common-land, of open spaces. This is because land is so *dear*. Why is land dear, John Smith? I will tell you by and bye.

The chief causes of the evils I have pointed out to you, John, are competition, monopoly, and bad management. There is a penny pamphlet, called " Milk and Postage Stamps," by " Elihu," sold by Abel Heywood. Read it. It shows you the waste of labour that comes of competition.

Go into any street and you will see two or three carts delivering milk. A cart, a pony, and a man to carry milk to a few houses ; and one postman serves a whole district ; as one milkman and one horse could, were it not for competition.

Again, in each house there is a woman cooking a dinner for one family, or washing clothes for one family. And the woman is over-worked, and the cooking is badly done, and the house is made horrible by steam and the odours of burnt fat. So with all the things we do and use. We have two grocers' shops next door to each other, each with a staff of servants, each with its own costly fixtures. Yet one big store would do as well, and would save half the cost and labour. Fancy a private post office in every street. How much would it cost to send a letter from Oldham to London?

So now let me tell you roughly what I suggest as an improvement on things as they now are.

First of all, I would restrict our mines, furnaces, chemical works, and factories to the number actually needed for the supply of our own people. Then I would stop the smoke nuisance by developing water power and electricity. Then I would set men to work to grow wheat and fruit and rear cattle and poultry for our own use. Then I would develop the fisheries and construct great fish-breeding lakes and harbours.

In order to achieve these ends I would make all the land, mills, mines, factories, works, shops, ships, and railways the property of the people.

I would have the towns rebuilt with wide streets, with detached houses, with gardens and fountains and avenues of trees. I would make the railways, the carriage of letters, and the transit of goods as free as the roads and bridges.

I would make the houses loftier and larger, and clear them of all useless furniture. I would institute public dining halls, public baths, public wash-houses on the best plans, and so set free the hands of those slaves—our English women.

I would have public parks, public theatres, music halls, gymnasiums, football and cricket fields, public halls and public gardens for recreation and music and refreshment. I would have all our children fed and clothed and educated at the cost of the State. I would have them all taught to play and to sing. I would have them all trained to athletics and to arms. I would have public halls of science. I would have the people become their own artists, actors, musicians, soldiers, and police. Then, by degrees, I would make all these things *free*. So that clothing, lodging, fuel, food, amusement, intercourse, education, and all the requirements for a perfect human life should be produced and distributed and enjoyed by the people without the use of money.

Now, Mr. John Smith, practical and hard-headed man, look upon the two pictures. You may think that mine represents a state of things that is unattainable; but you *must* own that it is much fairer than the picture of things as they are.

As to the possibility of doing what I suggest we will consider all that in a future chapter. At present ask yourself two questions:—

1. Is Modern England as happy as it might be?

2. Is *my* England—Merrie England—a better place than the England in which we now live?

CHAPTER VI.

THE chief struggle of your life, Mr. Smith, is the struggle to get a living. The chief object of these letters is to convince you of three facts:—

1. That with all your labour and anxiety you do not get a good living.
2. That you might and should get a good living with a third of the trouble you now take to keep out of a pauper's suit.

3. That though you worked twenty hours a day and piled the earth with wealth you could have no more than a good living out of all the wealth you produced.

Nature declares, Mr. Smith, that a man shall live temperately, or suffer for it; Nature also declares that a man shall not live very long. So that in the richest state a citizen can enjoy no more than a natural amount, and that a small one, of material things, nor can he enjoy those for many years.

In short, the material needs of life are few and easily supplied.

But the range of the spiritual and intellectual pleasures and capacities is very wide. That is to say that the pleasures and powers of the mind are practically boundless.

The *great* nation, Mr. Smith, is not the nation with the most wealth ; but the nation with the best men and women.

Now the best part of man is his mind, therefore the best men and women are those with the best minds.

But in this country, and at this time, the bulk of the people do not cultivate their minds.

We have here, Mr. Smith, in the untrained, unused minds of a noble race of people an immense power for greatness lying fallow, like an untilled field. This is a more serious natural loss, as I hope to show you, than if all our mines and farms had never been " opened up to commerce."

Well, my ideal, as I said before, is Frugality of Body and Opulence of Mind.

I propose to make our material lives simple ; to spend as little time and labour as possible upon the production of food, clothing, houses, and fuel, in order that we may have more leisure.

And I propose to employ that leisure in the enjoyment of life and the acquirement of knowledge.

It is as though I said, " You have in each day 24 hours. You give 8 hours to sleep, 10 or 12 to work (' earning a living '), and the rest, or most of it, to folly ; go, then, and of your sixteen waking hours spend but four in ' getting a living,' and the other twelve in pleasure and in learning."

Before I attempt to show you in detail how I think you might profitably spend your leisure time, allow me to call your attention to some of the ways in which you now waste your time ; yes, and waste your labour also.

We will begin by a brief inquiry into the ordinary domestic waste of time and labour and money that goes on in an average working-class home.

In my last letter I spoke of the drudgery of Mrs. Smith's life. You know that each family has its own dinner cooked daily ; that each wife has her own washing day and baking day ; that she has her own cooking range and implements ; and that she makes a special journey to the shops once a day, or once a week, and buys her food and other necessaries in small quantities.

Take a working-class street of one hundred houses. Consider the waste therein. For the convenience of one hundred families you have

> One hundred small inconvenient wash-kitchens.
> One hundred ditto ditto ovens.
> One hundred ditto ditto drying-grounds.
> One hundred wringing machines—turned by hand.

You have one hundred dinners to cook every day. You have, every week, one hundred miserable washing days ; you have one hundred women going out to buy a pound of tea and sugar, or other trifles.

Consider the cost of the machines, the cost of coal, the labour and the trouble of the wives expended.

Now cast your eyes over these extracts. This is from " Problems of Poverty," by John A. Hobson, M.A. (Methuen, 2s. 6d.) :—

The poor, partly of necessity, partly by habit, make their purchases in minute quantities. A single family has been known to make *seventy-two* distinct purchases of tea within seven weeks, and the average purchases of a number of poor families for the same period amount to twenty-seven. Their groceries are bought largely by the ounce, their meat or fish by the half-pennyworth, their coal by the hundredweight, or even by the pound

This is from the same book :—

Astounding facts are adduced as to the prices paid by the poor for common articles of consumption, especially for vegetables, dairy produce, groceries, and coal. The price of fresh vegetables, such as carrots, parsnips, &c., in East London is not infrequently *ten times the price* at which the same articles can be purchased wholesale from the growers.

This is from " The Co-operative Movement To-day," by G. J. Holyoake (Methuen, 2s. 6d.) :—

It may be assumed that 100 shops earn on an average £2 a week, or £100 a year ; thus the hundred shops would earn £10,000 a year. Thus it is evident that every 4,000 poor families in a town *actually pay £10,000 a year* for having their humble purchases handed to them over a counter.

And Mr. Holyoake proceeds to show how by establishing one great central store the great bulk of this loss would be saved.

I said to you, when I began these articles, that I am a practical man, and speak from what I have seen. I know all about those small purchases, and big prices. I have picked up half-a-dozen empty bottles off as many ash-pits, when a child, and sold them for a penny to buy coal. I have gone out many a time to buy a quarter of an ounce of tea, and a farthing's worth of milk. They taught stern lessons in my school, John.

Now let me describe a different kind of experience, in a different school.

A company of soldiers numbers from eighty to a hundred men. The allowance of food to each man is ¾lb. of meat and 1lb. of bread. But besides that each man pays 3d. a day for "groceries," consisting of tea, coffee, milk, vegetables, and extra bread.

Now, if each man had a separate kitchen and cooked his own meals, that would mean a great waste of room and money and time, and it would also mean very poor feeding.

But each company strikes a man off duty as cook, and there is a general kitchen, where the cooks of the whole, or sometimes half the battalion prepare the meals. The result is better and cheaper messing and less labour and dirt.

Take, again, the case of a sergeants' mess. The sergeants have the same ration—1lb. of bread and ¾lb. of meat a day, and they pay about 6d. a day for "messing." One sergeant is appointed "caterer," and his duty is to expend the messing money and superintend the messing. He is, in fact, a kind of temporary landlord, or club-steward.

Now, I often filled that place, and I found that when, as occurred on detachment, we had only five or six sergeants in mess, it was very difficult to feed them on the money; but at headquarters, with thirty in mess, we could live well and afford luxuries, on the same allowance per head.

With these facts in our mind let us go back to our Manchester street of one hundred working-class families. Suppose, instead of keeping up the wasteful system I described, we abolish all those miserable and imperfect

drying-grounds, wringing machines, wash kitchens, and kitchen ranges, and arrange the street on communal lines.

We set up one laundry, with all the best machinery; we set up one big drying field; we set up one great kitchen, one general dining hall, and one pleasant tea garden. Then we buy all the provisions and other things in large quantities, and we appoint certain wives as cooks and laundresses, or, as is the case with many military duties, we let the wives take the duties in turn. Don't you see how much better and how much cheaper the meals would be? Don't you see how much easier the lives of our poor women would be? Don't you see how much more comfortable our homes would be? Don't you see how much more sociable and friendly we should become?

So with the housework when we had simple houses and furniture. Imagine the difference between the cleaning of all the knives by a rapid knife machine turned by an engine, and the drudgery of a hundred wives scrubbing at a hundred clumsy knife-boards.

I need not go into greater detail; you can elaborate the idea for yourself. Let us now turn from domestic to commercial waste.

Commercial waste is something appalling. The cause of commercial waste is competition. The chief channels of commercial waste are account-keeping, bartering, and advertising. If we produced goods simply for *use* instead of for sale, we should save all this waste. But consider the immense number of cashiers, book-keepers, clerks, salesmen, shopmen, accountants, commercial travellers, agents, and advertisement canvassers employed in our British trade.

Take the one item of advertisement alone. There are draughtsmen, paper-makers, printers, bill-posters, painters, carpenters, gilders, mechanics, and a perfect army of other people all employed in making advertisement bills, pictures, hoardings, and other abominations—for *what?*

To enable one soap or patent medicine dealer to secure more orders than his rival. I believe I am well within the mark when I say that some firms spend £100,000 a year in advertisements.

And who pays it, John? *You* pay it; *you*, the practical, hard-headed, shrewd British workman. You pay for everything, you silly fellow.

There is another element of waste which consists in the production of useless things, Mr. Smith; but of that I will speak at another time.

I will also show you, in a future letter, how the same competition which causes waste causes also a wicked obstruction of progress. At present just consider these questions. Why do gas companies oppose the establishment of electric-lighting companies? Is it because they think gas is the better light? Hey, John?

I said just now that we would consider the question of how to employ the leisure we should secure in a well-ordered state. Let us get an idea what that leisure would be.

At present less than one-third of the population are engaged in producing necessaries. This one-third of the people produce enough necessaries for all.

Now take the sum in two ways. If one-third produce enough for all, then three-thirds will produce three times as much as we need. Or, if one-third produce enough for all by working nine hours a day, then three-thirds will produce enough for all by working three hours a day.

So we shall have plenty of leisure. What are we to do with it?

One use for it is the acquirement of knowledge. I will give you two very striking examples of the kind of work that needs doing.

Take first, the Germ theory of disease. I am a very ignorant man, John, and can only offer hints. Read this:—

If the particular microbe of each contagious disease were known, the conditions of its life and activity understood, and the circumstances destructive of its life ascertained, there is great probability that its multiplication might be arrested, and the disease caused by it be abolished.

Consumption, typhoid and typhus fevers, cholera, and many other plagues are spread by small creatures called microbes. At present we do not know enough about these microbes to exterminate them. That is *one* thing well worth finding out.

Take next the subject of agricultural chemistry. Read this:—

In studying the utilisation of vegetable products for obtaining the various animal matters which are used as food, &c., agricultural chemistry enters into a higher and more difficult field. Although many useful practical results have been obtained this department of our knowledge is extremely incomplete.

You remember what I told you about the yield of the land. Given a thorough knowledge of agricultural chemistry and there is no doubt that we might produce more food with less labour. So that is *another* thing worth knowing.

Now I know your absurd modesty, John Smith, and how ready you are to despise your own efforts; and I can almost *hear* you saying, "what can ignorant men like us do in these difficult sciences?"

But John, I don't flatter you, as you know, but you have brains, and *good* brains, if you only had the chance to use them. Sometimes a few of you *do* get a chance to use them. There was William Smith, the greatest English geologist, he was a poor farmer's son, and chiefly self-taught; there was Sir William Herschel, the great astronomer, he played the oboe in a watering-place band; there were Faraday, the bookbinder, and Sir Humphrey Davy, the apothecary's apprentice, both great scientists; there were James Watt the mathematical instrument maker, and George Stephenson the collier, and Arkwright the barber, and Jacquard the weaver, and John Hunter the great anatomist, who was a poor Scotch carpenter. Those men did some good in science; and why not others?

Ah! Why not? That is the question. The common people are like an untilled, unwatered, and unweeded garden. No one has yet studied or valued the capacities of men. We know that some few of the Hunter and Herschel stamp have come out well, and some of us think that when a man has brains he *must* come out well; but that is a mistake. Only here and there, John, chiefly by good luck, does one of our clever poor men succeed in being useful, and in developing his force or part of it.

I will speak from personal experience. I know several men, poor and unknown, who have in them great capacity. I have now in my mind's eye a young Lancashire man, who *might* have been a very fine writer. But he is poor, and he has no knowledge of writing, no knowledge of style or grammar, and if he had would find it very difficult to get work.

I once knew a blacksmith, a man of strong character, of great probity, a born orator, a man of intellect. Often I have heard him, as he beat on the red iron, beat out also, in rough homely language, most beautiful and forcible thoughts. John, he could not read or write. He was of middle-age, he had a large family, he did not suspect that he was clever.

Take my own case. I became a writer by accident—by a series of accidents—and not that until I was thirty-four. And I have done fairly well, and have been very lucky. But I am sure I should have done better at a quite different kind of work. And I am sure that if my mother had not taught me to read and encouraged me to love literature I should never have been a writer at all.

But suppose, John Smith, my mother had died when my father died, or suppose she had been an ignorant woman, or a careless one. Where would Nunquam have gone to? He would probably be now in the grave, or in a prison. Yet he would have taken with him to the churchyard or the treadmill the same mind that is now struggling with this task—a task too great for it—the task of persuading John Smith, of Oldham, to do his duty as a husband, as a father, as a citizen, and as a man.

So, John, consider, John, what chance have the poor? Education is so dear. The sciences and the arts are locked up, and the privileged classes hold the key; and down in Ancoats and the Seven Dials the wretched mothers feed our young Faradays and Miltons on gin, and send them out ignorant and helpless to face the winter wind and the vice and disease of the stews.

It makes me angry when I think of it, and I must be calm and practical, because you, John Smith, are such a shrewd hard-headed man—God help you.

John, John Smith, of Oldham, remember what noble men and women have come from the ranks of the common people.

Now, John, at present the working people of this country live under conditions altogether monstrous. Their labour is much too heavy, their pleasures are too few, and in their close streets and crowded houses decency and health and cleanliness are well nigh impossible.

It is not only the wrong of this that I resent, it is the *waste.* Look through the slums, John, and see what childhood, girlhood, womanhood, and manhood have there become. Think what a waste of beauty, of virtue, of strength, and of all the power and goodness that go to make a nation great is being consummated there by ignorance and by injustice.

For, depend upon it every one of our brothers or sisters ruined or slain by poverty or vice, is a loss to the nation of so much bone and sinew, of so much courage and skill, of so much glory and delight.

Cast your eyes, then, John Smith the practical, over the Registrar-General's returns, and imagine if you can how many gentle nurses, good mothers, sweet singers, brave soldiers, and clever artists, inventors, and thinkers are swallowed up every year in that ocean of crime and sorrow, which is known to the official mind as " The high death-rate of the wage-earning classes."

Alas, John, the pity of it.

Well, I want to stop that waste, my practical friend. I want to give those cankered flowers light and air, and clear their roots of weeds.

And in *my* " Merrie England " there will be great colleges for the study of science, and the training of the *people,* so that the whole force of the national mind may be brought to bear upon those important questions of agriculture, of manufactures, and of medicine, which are now but partly understood, because it is the rich and not the clever who consider them, and because *they* only work selfishly and secretly, in opposition instead of in mutual helpfulness.

CHAPTER VII.

NOW, John, what are the evils of which we complain? Lowness of wages, length of working hours, uncertainty of employment, insecurity of the future, low standards of public health and morality, prevalence of pauperism and crime, and the existence of false ideals of life.

I will give you a few examples of the things I mean. It is estimated that in this country, with its population of thirty-six millions, there are generally about 700,000 men out of work. There are about 800,000 paupers. Of every thousand persons who die in Merrie England over nine hundred die without leaving any property at all. About eight millions of people exist always on the borders of destitution. About twenty millions are poor. More than half the national income belongs to about ten thousand people. About thirty thousand people own fifty-five fifty-sixths of the land and capital of the kingdom, but of thirty-six millions of people only 1½ millions get above £3 a week. The average income per head of the working classes is about £17 a year, or less than 1s. a day. There are millions of our people working under conditions and living in homes that are simply disgraceful. The sum of crime, vice, drunkenness, gambling, prostitution, idleness, ignorance, want, disease, and death is appalling.

These are facts. They are facts which stare us in the face in every town, and at all hours of the day and night. They are facts so well known that I need not rake the Blue Books for statistics to confirm them. I wish to use as few figures as possible. I also wish to avoid angry words. Therefore, Mr. Smith, I simply point out these evils and ask you as a practical and honest man whether you don't think they ought to be remedied.

To what are the above evils due? They are due to the unequal distribution of wealth, and to the absence of justice and order from our society.

Consider, first, the distribution of the annual earnings. The following figures are given on the authority of Giffen, Levi, and Mulholland.

	£.
Gross national earnings	1,350,000,000
Amount paid in rent	220,000,000
Amount paid in interest	270,000,000
Salaries of middle-classes and profits of employers, &c.	360,000,000
Wages of the working classes	500,000,000

That is to say, the workers earn 1,350 millions. Of that the Rich take, in rent and interest, 490 millions, and the Rich and Middle-classes, in profits and salaries, take another 360 millions, or a total of 850 millions, leaving for the working classes little more than one-third (500 millions).

Now for the proportions. As I said just now, there are less than 1½ millions who pay income tax on incomes of £150 a year and upwards. Multiply 1½ millions by 3 and you get 4½ millions as the gross number of men, women, and children of the middle and upper classes. Four-and-a-half millions will be just one-eighth of our population. Thus we find that 850 millions go to one-eighth of the population, and 500 millions to the other seven-eighths.

Speaking in round numbers the averages *per head* are as follow :—

> Middle and upper classes, per year, £184.
> Working classes, per year, £16.

The following diagram will give you an idea of the inequality of this division :—

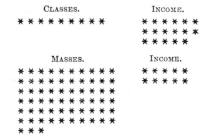

But this is not the worst. Besides the fact that the upper and middle classes take nearly two-thirds of the wealth which the masses earn, there is the fact that those classes, and probably less than a tenth of those classes, actually own all the land and all the instruments by which wealth can be produced.

Political orators and newspaper editors are very fond of talking to you about "your country." Now, Mr. Smith, it is a hard practical fact that you have not got any country. The British Islands do not belong to the British people; they belong to a few thousands—certainly not half a million—of rich men.

These men not only own the land, they own, also, the rivers and lakes, the mines and minerals, the farms and orchards, the trees and thickets; the cattle and horses, and sheep and pigs, and poultry and game; the mills, factories, churches, houses, shops, railways, trains, ships, machinery, and, in fact, nearly everything except the bodies and souls of the workers, and, as I will try to show you, they have almost complete power over these.

Yes, not only do the rich own the land, and all the buildings and machinery, but also, and because they own those things, they have reduced the workers to a condition of dependence.

For you know very well, Mr. Smith, that it is true of nearly all our working men that they cannot work when they choose to work, but must first find a rich man—a capitalist— who is willing to employ them.

This is because the capitalists own the land and the tools. What can the ploughman do without the land and the plough; or the collier without the pit and the machinery; or the weaver without the loom and factory?

You know that in these days of machinery there are hardly any men who own the tools of their own trade. And if they did they would be helpless; for they must sell their work in a market where the capitalist competes with them, and where he will undersell them, even if he loses by the sale, and so make it impossible for them to live.

Rent, interest, private ownership, machinery and competition, are all instruments in the hands of the capitalist, and with those instruments he compels the worker to give up nearly all his earnings in return for permission to work.

You are an agricultural labourer. I own a piece of land. You come to me and beg for "work." I "engage" you at 15s. a week, and all you produce is *mine*. You are a slave, for if you quit my employ you must starve; and although I have no whip or chain, I have that which serves as well to compel you to work hard, that is to say, I have the power to turn you off the land. So if you are a cotton operative, and I own a cotton mill. You must come to me and ask for work. If I refuse it you must starve. If I offer it you must take it at my price. Oh, yes, you can form a trade union, and strike, refusing to accept my price. In that case I may give you rather more than I offered, because it will pay me better to let you have half the money you earn and be content myself with the other half than to let you remain idle and so make nothing by you at all. But you know I can always beat you, for I have enough to live upon in idleness, and you have *nothing*.

Well, it is true that the land and all the mines, mills, houses, and machinery—that is to say, the "Land" and "Capital"—of this country are owned by a few rich people. And it is urged in defence of this private ownership of the "means of livelihood" that, in the first place, the rich have a "right" to their possessions; and, in the second place, that the rich use these possessions to the general advantage.

Both these statements are untrue.

First, as to the rich man's "right" to his wealth. I suppose that you, as a sensible and honest man, will admit this principle: viz., that a man has a "right" to that which he has produced by the unaided exercise of his own faculties; but that he has *not* a right to that which is not produced by his own unaided faculties; nor to the whole of that which has been produced by his faculties aided by the faculties of another man.

If you admit the above principle, then I think I can prove to you that no man has a right to the private ownership of a single square foot of land; and that no man could of his own efforts produce more private property than is commonly possessed by a monkey or a bear.

We will begin with the land; and you will find that the original title to all the land possessed by private owners is the title of conquest, or theft.

There are four chief ways in which land may become private property. It may be confiscated by force; it may be filched by fraud; it may be received as a gift; or it may be bought with money.

Of the land held by our rich peers the greater part has been plundered from the church, stolen from the common-lands, or received in gifts from the crown. If you will buy a little book called " Our Old Nobility," price 1s., published by H. Vickers, Strand, London, you will begin to have an idea of the ways in which our " noble " families got possession of their estates. From that book I quote the following lines :—

The Fitzroys are certainly descended from one of the vilest of women: Barbara Palmer, wife of Lord Castlemaine, and mistress of Charles II. . . . One of Charles's Ministers was Henry Bennet, Earl of Arlington, whose only daughter was married at the mature age of twelve to young Fitzroy, the son of Barbara Palmer and Charles II. Ample provision was made for the young couple. In 1673 Charles granted to the Earl of Arlington for life, and to Fitzroy and his wife afterwards, a very extensive tract of Crown land, viz., the lordship and manor of Grafton, manor of Hartwell, and lands in Hartwell, Roade, and Hanslope, manors of Alderton, Blisworth, Stoke Bruerne, Green's Norton, Potterspury, Ashton, Paulerspury, part of Charcomb Priory, lands in Grimscott, Houghton Parva, Northampton, Hardingston, and Shuttlehanger, parcel of Sewardsley Priory, the office and fee of the honour of Grafton, and the forests of Salcey and Whittlebury (reserving the timber to the Crown). This extraordinary grant will account for the large estates of the Fitzroys in Northamptonshire and Bucks. The Fitzroys inherit their Suffolk estates from the Earl of Arlington. This patriotic statesman, who formed one of the notorious Cabal Ministry, not content with taking bribes from the King of France, and with the lucrative posts of Secretary of State, Keeper of the Privy Purse, and Postmaster-General, managed to secure for himself a number of valuable grants, as is shown by the State Papers in the Record Office, among which were a moiety of the estates of a former Earl of Lenox, and several manors in the county of Wicklow. He also obtained a lease of Marylebone Park on advantageous terms, and another lease of three-fourths of Great St. John's Wood at an annual rental of £21 6s. 2d. No wonder that he was able to purchase Euston Hall and the surrounding lands. One of his Suffolk lordships was formerly part of the possessions of St. Edmund's Abbey, though whether acquired by grant or purchase is not clear. Charles II. was not content with giving away Crown lands in the wholesale manner above described; the children of his harlots were further provided for at the public expense. The Duke of Grafton, for instance, had an

hereditary pension of £9,000 a year granted from the Excise, and £4,700 a year from the Post Office, which continued to be paid till a comparatively recent date. The former pension was redeemed in 1858 by a payment of £193,777, and the latter in 1856 by a payment of £91,181. There was also a very lucrative sinecure in the family, which the Duke of Grafton surrendered in 1795 for an annuity of £870 a year—an arrangement ratified by the Act 46 Geo. III., cap. 89.

I want you to read that book, John, and also Henry George's "Progress and Poverty," 1s., published by Paul, Trench, Trübner and Co., London.

But leaving the men who have stolen the land, or got it by force, or fraud, let us consider the title of those who have bought the land.

Many people have bought land, and paid for it. Have they a right to it ?

No. They have no right to that land, and for these two reasons.

1. They bought it of someone who had no right to sell it.
2. They paid for it with money which they themselves had never earned.

Land, you will observe, Mr. Smith, is the gift of Nature. It is not made by man. Now, if a man has a right to nothing but that which he has himself made, no man can have a right to the land, for no man made it.

It would be just as reasonable for a few families to claim possession of the sea and the air, and charge their fellow creatures rent for breathing or bathing, as it is for those few families to grab the land and call it theirs. As a matter of fact, John, we are charged for breathing, for without a sufficient space of land to breathe on we cannot get good air to breathe.

If a man claimed the sea, or the air, or the light as his, you would laugh at his presumption, Mr. Smith. Now, I ask you to point out to me any reason for private ownership of land which will not act as well as a reason for private ownership of sea and air.

So we may agree that no man can have any *right* to the land. And if a man can have no right to the land, how can he have a right to sell the land ? And if I buy a piece of land from one who has no right to sell it, how can I call that land mine ?

Take a case. William the Conqueror stole

an estate from Harold (to whom it did not belong) and gave it to a Norman Baron. During the Wars of the Roses said Baron lost it to another Baron, or to the crown. Later on the estate is confiscated by Charles II. and given to a bastard son of his. The descendants of that bastard son take to gambling and lose the estate to the Jews. The Jews sell it to a wealthy cotton-lord.

But the land is stolen property, and the cotton-lord is a receiver of stolen property.

Suppose a footpad knocked down a traveller and stole his watch. Gave the watch to his sweetheart, who sold it to a Jew, who sold it again to a sailor, and suppose the traveller came forward and claimed his watch. Would the law let the sailor keep it ? No. But if the footpad had been made a peer for stealing it *that* would have made a difference.

You may say, of course, that the law of the land has confirmed the old nobility in the possession of their stolen property. That is quite true. But it is equally true that the law was made by the landowners themselves. In the eighteenth century the big landowners robbed the small landowners in a shameful and wholesale way. Within a space of about eighty years no less than 7,000,000 acres were " enclosed."

And when we suggest that the land of England should be restored to the English people from whom it was stolen, these landrobbers have the impudence to raise the cry of " plunder."

Here, for instance, is an extract from a Tory evening paper, cut by me some years ago :—

The impudent agitators who suggest the confiscation of the land, are dumb as to the rights and services of the landowner. They ignore the facts that the land is his, and that if he administers the estate he chiefly creates its value.

The land is *not* " his." Man has a right only to what his labour makes. No man " makes " the land.

The nobleman does *not*—in most cases— administer his estate. The estate is managed by farmers, who pay the nobleman a heavy rent for being allowed to do his work.

Therefore the landlord does *not* " create the value " of the estate. The value of an estate consists in the industry of those who work upon it. To say that Lord Blankdash has farm lands or town property worth £50,000 a year means that he has the legal power to take that money from the factory hands and farmworkers for the use of that which is as much theirs as his.

I suppose you are aware, Mr. Smith, that no " value " can be got out of an estate without labour If you doubt this, take a nineacre field, fence it in, and wait until it grows crops. You know it will *never* grow crops, unless someone ploughs it and sows it.

No : even if you have land and capital you cannot raise a single ear of corn without labour. Take your nine-acre field. Put in a steam plough, a sack of seed, a harrow, and a bank-book, and wait for crops. You will not get a stalk of corn. A poor labourer with a broken shovel and a piece of thorn bush will raise more wheat in his little patch of back garden than all the capital of England could get out of all the acres of Europe without labour.

But read the following report of a land company, taken from the *Pall Mall Gazette* in 1891 :—

SWAZILAND GOLD EXPLORATION AND LAND COMPANY.

The annual general meeting of this company was held this afternoon at Winchester House. Mr. E. A. Pontifex, the chairman, presided, and moved the adoption of the report. He said that since the last meeting practically nothing had been done. *They had been waiting for more prosperous times.* They were an exploring and land, not a mining company, with a view to inducing others to form subsidiary companies for working the property. At the present moment the formation of companies was practically a dead letter ; and it would be useless to point out to promoters where operations could be carried on, as they would be unable to raise the necessary funds to carry on the works. They had reduced the expenses to the lowest possible limit, the directors having foregone their fees, and the total amount being only £400 a year. *They were awaiting better times, and the advent of railways,* before endeavouring to work the riches they believed were contained *in the 156 square miles of territory which they possessed.* Since their last meeting, the High Court of Swaziland, sitting at Kremersdorp, had confirmed the concession originally made by the late King Umbandine, and it was held to by the King's successors and the Boer Republic and the English Government, which now prevails in Swaziland. Nor was it likely that any further call would be made until the arrival of more enterprising times.

The italics are mine. The company owns 156 square miles of land; and it does not pay them a cent! Why? Because there is no labour on it. The company are waiting for railways. Why? Because railways will carry people out there. Mines, farms, towns, will come into existence. The pick and the plough will go to work, and then—*then* the Swaziland square miles will be *valuable*. In other words, the men who make the wealth in Swaziland will have to pay a lot of it to the English company as rent for the land the company have "acquired."

The case above given is clear enough for the capacity of a child. There is the whole problem made plain. Labour and capital: Labour and land. One hundred and fifty-six square miles of land, and not a shilling return. Not so much as comes back from the land on which is built an Ancoats slum cottage. But a man *lives* in the cottage; and he works, and a part of his earnings goes unto the " owner " of the land. Do you see it *now*, Mr. Smith?

Have you ever considered the question of house rent? Suppose you own a cottage in a country village, and I own a cottage of the same size in a busy town, close to a big railway and a number of factories. You know that I shall get more rent for my house than you will get for yours. Why?

Because my house stands on more desirable land. The railway company would buy it. And then it is near to places of work, and workmen will pay more for it, especially as houses are scarce.

But did I make the railway? Did I build the factories? Did I do *anything* to make the wealth of the town, or the " value " of the land? Not I. The workers did that, and so I am paid for what they did. That is to say, I am allowed, by raising my rent, to put a tax upon their industry.

The poor wretches in the East End of London pay from 3s. to 6s. a week for one small room in a weather-worn and dirty house, in a narrow and unhealthy street; and rents in Manchester are high. This is owing to the value of the land. That is to say, the people are forced by stress of circumstances not only to live in the rotten nests of these pestilential rookeries, but have no option but to give the extortionate prices demanded by landlords whose bowels of compassion are dried up, and whose souls are shrunken by the fires of avarice.

Land is "valuable"—that is, tenants will submit to be cheated—in all centres of industry. The skill, the energy, and the orderliness of the workers create an " industrial centre." Speculators buy land near that centre, and as business and work draw people thereto in search of a living, the " speculator " raises his prices and grows rich, and his land and houses are " valuable " This is according to the law It constitutes a dishonest and an unreasonable tax on labour, but it is lawful. There is in it neither principle nor humanity—but it is the law; and the difficulty of improving the dwellings of the people lies in the fact that you cannot alter this law without damaging the sacred rights of property.

Do you ever think about these things? Do you know the difference between the land law and the patent laws and copyright?

A nobleman owns an estate. He draws £30,000 in rent from it annually. He and his family before him have drawn that rent for five or six centuries, and the land is still his.

But if John Smith of Oldham invents a new loom and patents it, his patent right expires in about twenty-one years. For twenty-one years he may reap the fruits of his cleverness. At the end of that time anyone may work his patent without charge. It has become public property. This is the law.

Or John Smith of Oldham writes a book. The book is copyright for forty years, or for the life of the author and seven years after. Whilst it is copyright no one can print the book without John's leave, and so John may make money by his cleverness. But at the end of that time the copyright lapses and the book becomes public property Anyone may print it then.

Now you see the difference between land law and patent law. The landlord's patent *never* runs out. The land *never* becomes public property. The rent is perpetual. And yet the landlord did not make the land; whereas John Smith *did* invent the loom.

Mr. Smith, if you *are* a practical hard-headed man, I think I may leave you to study the land question for yourself.

CHAPTER VIII.

WE have now, Mr. Smith, to consider a very important question, viz., have the rich any *right* to their riches ?

I have already laid it down as my guiding principle that a man has a right to all the wealth that he creates by the exercise of his own unaided faculties ; and to no more.

If you look into my pamphlet, "The Pope's Socialism," page 4, you will find the following paragraph :—

No man has any right to *be* rich. No man ever yet became rich by fair means. No man ever became rich by his own industry.

That statement, "no man ever became rich by his own industry," has puzzled many of my readers, and I shall explain it.

I shall explain it because, if no man can become rich by his own industry, then no man has a right to be rich at all.

How do men grow rich ? In these days the three chief sources of wealth are :—

1. Rent.
2. Interest.
3. Profits.

First, Rent. Who earns it ? We will take two examples : Ground Rent, and Property Rent.

The Duke of Plaza Toro owns an estate. The rent roll is £30,000 a year. Where does the money come from ?

The estate is let out to farmers, at so much per acre. These farmers pay the duke his £30,000 a year. Where do the farmers get it from ?

The farmers sell their crops, and out of the purchase money pay the rent. How are the crops raised ?

The crops are raised by the agricultural labourers, under the direction of the farmers.

That is to say, that the rent is earned by labour—by the labour of the farmer and his men. The duke does nothing. The duke did not make the land, nor does he raise the crops. He has therefore no *right* to take the rent at all

The man who gets rich on ground rent gets rich on the labour of others.

Mr. Bounderby owns a row of houses. The rental of the street amounts to £400 a year. Where does the money come from ?

The rent is paid by the tenants of the houses. It is paid with money they have earned by their labour, or with money which they have obtained from other men who earned it by their labour, and it is paid to Mr. Bounderby for the use of his houses.

How did Mr. Bounderby get his houses ? He either bought them with money which he did not earn by his own industry, or he paid for the material and the building with money which he did not earn by his own industry.

Two things are quite certain. First, that Mr. Bounderby did not build the houses with his own hands, nor make the bricks and timbers of which they are built ; that work was done by other men. And second, that the money with which those men were paid was never earned by Mr. Bounderby's own industry.

Mr. Bounderby has therefore no right to own those houses or to charge rent for them.

The man who grows rich upon house rents grows rich upon the labour of others.

But you will very properly ask, Mr. Smith, how I prove that the money paid by Mr. Bounderby for his houses was not earned by his own industry.

This brings us to the second and third means by which men get wealth : Interest and profits.

What is interest ? It is money paid for the use of money. If you lent me a hundred pounds at 5 per cent. interest, that would mean that I must pay you five pounds a year for the loan of the money as long as I kept it, and that such payment would not reduce the amount of the loan. So that if I kept your £100 for twenty years and paid you £5 a year interest, I should at the end of that time still owe you £100. That is to say, you would receive £200 from me, although you only lent me £100.

Where do I get the interest from ? I have to work for it. But you get it from me. You don't work for it. You—possibly—worked for the principal, that is, for the first hundred pounds; but you do not work for the interest, the second hundred pounds.

Suppose I have £1,000. I put it in a bank and draw 3 per cent., £30 a year, interest for it. At the end of twenty years I shall have drawn out £600, and yet there will be £1,000 to my credit. How does my money breed money? How do I get £1,600 for £1,000? How can the banker afford to pay me more than I put into the bank?

If instead of putting my £1,000 into a bank I locked it up in a safe, and drew out £30 a year for twenty years, would there be £1,000 left at the end of that time? There would not. There would only be £400. Money does *not* breed money. Interest has to be worked for. Who *earns* it?

Suppose a rich Jew has lent a million to the Government at 3 per cent. He draws every year £30,000 in interest. Who pays it? It is raised by taxation. Who pays the taxes? They are all paid either by the workers or by those who get their money from the workers. And the Jew gets his interest *for ever*. That is to say, that after he has drawn back all his million in interest the Government goes on paying him out of your earnings, my hard-headed friend, £30,000 a year as long as any one is left to claim it. Probably the million was wasted in some foolish work, or wicked war; but because a Minister in 1812 was a knave or a fool, British industry is taxed to the tune of £30,000 a year, world without end, amen.

And the worst of it is that the money the Jew lent was not earned by him, but by the ancesters of the very people who are now paying his descendants interest for the loan of it.

Nay: Worse even than this. It is a fact that a great deal of the so-called "capital" for which interest is paid, *does not exist at all.*

The Duke of Plaza Toro is a wealthy peer. He has an income, a rent-roll of £30,000 a year. The Earl of Chow Bent has £40,000 a year, the Marquis of Steyne has £50,000 a year. These noblemen, together with a rich Jew, a couple of rich cotton-lords, and a coal owner, decide to form a company and construct a canal.

They engage some engineers and some navvies. To pay these men their wages and to provide tools and other "plant," they need "capital."

They get an estimate of the cost. Say it is half a million. The capital of the company is half a million. But that is needed to *complete* the work. It can be started with much less. They therefore issue 50,000 shares at £10 each; £2 payable on allotment, and the rest at stated times.

The company consists of seven men. Each takes an equal number of shares, each pays down an equal sum, say £14,285, making a total of £100,004. With this amount they can go on until the second call is made.

Now look at the position of the Duke. He has paid in his £14,000, and at the end of a year he will have another £30,000 ready, in the shape of *rent*. The others are in similar positions. The Jew waits for his *interest*, the coal-owner and the cotton lords for their *profits*. And all these sums, the rent, the interest, and the profits, are earned by the workers.

So the canal is made. Who makes it? Not the rich share-owners. Oh, no. The canal is made by the engineers and the navvies. And who finds the money? Not the rich share-holders. Oh, no. The money is earned in rent, or interest, or profits, by the agricultural labourers, the colliers, and the cotton operatives.

But when the navvies and engineers have made the canal, and when the labourers, miners, and spinners have paid for it, who owns it?

Does it belong to the men who made it? Not at all. Does it belong to the men who earned the money to pay for it? Not at all.

It belongs to the rich share-holders, and these men will get other men to work it, and will keep the profits of its working.

That is to say, all the goods which are carried on that canal must pay tollage. This tollage, after the costs of repairing and working the canal are defrayed, will be profit, and will be divided amongst the share-holders in the form of dividends. Who will pay the tollage?

The tollage will be paid by the people who

carry the goods, and they in turn will charge it to the people who buy the goods, and they in turn will charge it to the people who *use* the goods. And the people who use the goods will be either workers, who pay the toll out of their own earnings, or rich people, who pay the toll out of the earnings of other workers.

And now let us sum up.

The Duke of Plaza Toro lends £14,000 which he has got (out of his farm labourers) and £56,000 which he has *not* got, but which he *will* get *as soon as his farm labourers have earned it.* With this money—the money earned and to be earned by the farm labourers —the duke pays wages to the engineers and navvies who make the canal.

The canal being made, the Duke takes tollage, which is paid by the workers, much of it, perhaps, by the farm labourers, navvies, engineers, spinners, and colliers, who found the money for the canal or did the work of making it.

That is to say, the workers pay the Duke interest for the loan of their own money.

You will begin, now, Mr. Smith, to see what is meant by such words as Rent, Interest, Capital, and Credit. For your further enlightenment, and to give you an idea how poor these rich men really are, and how very much interest is paid for money which does not exist, let me offer you two facts.

The first fact is that whereas the amount annually paid in wages, profits, interest, and rent is estimated at £1,350,000,000, there is at no time as much as £100,000,000 of *money* in the country.

The second fact I will give you in the words of John Stuart Mill :—

When men talk of the ancient wealth of a country, of riches inherited from ancestors. and similar expressions, the idea suggested is, chat the riches so transmitted were produced long ago, at the time when they are said to have been first acquired, and that no portion of the capital of a country was produced this year, except so much as may have been this year added to the total amount. The fact is far otherwise.

The greater part, in value, of the wealth now existing in England has been produced by human hands within the last twelve months. A very small proportion indeed of that large aggregate was in existence ten years ago; of the present productive

capital of the country scarcely any part, except farm houses and factories, and a few ships and machines; and even these would not in most cases have survived so long, if fresh labour had not been employed within that period in putting them into repair.

The land subsists, and the land is almost the only thing that subsists. Everything which is produced perishes, and most things very quickly.

And again :—

Capital is kept in existence from age to age, not by preservation, but by perpetual reproduction.

Does that surprise you, John Smith? Nearly all the boasted "capital" or wealth of the rich is produced *annually.*

And by *whom* is it produced, John? By the rich? Not at all. It is produced by those who labour, for *all* wealth *must* be produced by labour. By no other means can it be produced.

You hear a man described as a millionaire. Do you suppose that he has a million or a hundred million pounds in his safe? Do you imagine with regard to a Jay Gould or a Duke of Westminster that every year a million golden coins rain down on him from Heaven?

Your millionaire has hardly anything. Very little money, that is certain. But he has bonds and securities and other written contrivances of the usurer and the devil, whereby he is legally entitled to appropriate year by year some millions of the wealth that is created by the labour of the poor.

Your Duke of Plaza Toro is said to be worth £500,000 a year. How is he worth it? He gets it in rent, in royalties, in dividends, in interest ; and every penny of it is taken from the wealth produced by labour.

Your Duke has £30,000 a year of a rent-roll, has he? But he has not a shilling of rent until poor Hodge has raised the crops and farmer Giles has sold them. Take the men, the labourers—poor despised drudges— off his Grace's estates, and his Grace is a pauper.

I advise, you, John, to get a pamphlet called "Society Classified : In reply to the question, 'How far is the saying true that every one lives either by working or begging, or by stealing?'" It is well worth your attention. The author is E. D. Girdlestone; the publisher is W. Reeves, 185, Fleet - street, London; the price, one penny.

CHAPTER IX.

THE next thing we have to discover, Mr. Smith, is, What is profit? Profit is the excess price received for an article over the price paid for it.

If a man sells a thing for more money than he buys it for the balance is profit.

You will see, then, that men may make profit either upon their own work or upon the work of others.

As a rule profit is not made by the producer of an article, but by some other person commonly called "the middleman" because he goes between the producer and the consumer; that is to say he, the middleman, buys the article from the maker, and sells it to the user, at a profit.

In some cases, and to some extent, this profit is fair. For example, a costermonger buys fish in the market, carries it into the city and sells it at a profit. That profit is his wage, and pays him for his work as a distributor or carrier of goods from the producer to the user.

But when the middleman becomes a capitalist; when he buys fish on the Kentish beach by the ton and sells it at a profit to the shopkeeper and the coster, making for himself a couple of thousand a year, while the fisherman and the coster can hardly keep body and soul together, that is not a fair profit at all.

Why? Just look at it in this light. Here are four persons concerned in the fishery trade.

1. The fisherman, or getter.
2. The middleman, or dealer.
3. The coster, or carrier.
4. The consumer, or user.

Now, can you see any *reason* why of these four people the middleman, who does nothing but sign cheques, should fare so much better than any of the others?

We have three persons engaged in getting the fish from the sea to our doors. Is it fair that he who does the least work should have the most money? Is the work done by, or rather done *for*, the middleman so much more valuable to the public than the work of the fisherman and the coster?

My dear John, the middleman's work, so far from being the most valuable of the three, is actually worse than useless.

The middleman in fact does nothing but keep up the price of fish and keep down the rate of wages by his exorbitant profits.

Put the case to yourself thus. Suppose you were contractor, or caterer, for the supply of food to an entire town. Would you pay a man £2,000 a year for simply ordering other men to send telegrams to local agents to buy fish on the beach? I don't think you would. Being a hard-headed person, you would pay a clerk the current rate of wages to do all that, and so would save at least £1,800 a year. You would see *then*, in a moment, that the middleman was a mere snatcher of profits, taking from the producer with one hand and from the consumer with the other.

Now, John, hold your breath and be brave.

All employers of labour, all rich men, except the money-lenders and the landlords, are middlemen.

They are all useless incumbrances, getting rich upon the labour of others.

There are three chief kinds of middlemen:

1. The idle capitalist, who pays men to work for him, and pays managers to direct them, but never works himself.
2. The busy capitalist who pays men to work for him, and himself directs and manages the sale of what they make.
3. The capitalistic worker, or inventor, who has invented some new process or machine, and who employs other men to make or work the patent.

The first of these men is worse than useless. The second is, or might be, useful, but is almost always very much overpaid. The third is sometimes an evil, sometimes a good, ought always to be valuable to any nation, and is the *only* kind of capitalist with any pretence of a right to his riches. His case we must consider very carefully.

When I said in "The Pope's Socialism" that no man ever became rich by his own industry. the inventor was instanced against me by some of my readers.

They could not see that a man who made a fortune out of an invention did not grow rich by his own industry.

Yet the fact is very clear.

We will suppose that you, John Smith, of Oldham, invent a new kind of loom, which will do twice as much work as any other kind of loom now known.

You *patent* that loom, and for twenty-one years exact a royalty upon every such loom that is made. Thus you grow rich.

Do you grow rich by your own industry? By your own unaided industry? Is all the machine your own invention? Does no other man's hand help you in the getting of your riches?

If you consider, Mr. Smith, you will find that you owe your invention to a legion of dead and nameless men ; and your wealth to a legion of poor workers of your own time.

First. Your loom contains wheels, and shafts, and pinions, and is worked by steam. Did *you* invent the wheel? Did *you* discover steam? No. They were there ready to your hand, invented, like the hammer and the file you used, and the principles of mechanics by which you worked, by men long dead; by men without whose labours your wonderful invention had never been.

But, again, of what is your loom made? Of iron, of copper, of steel ; of timber and many other materials. But you are not a miner, nor a puddler, nor a joiner, nor a smith or moulder.

So that to *invent* your machine you borrow from the dead ; and to make it you must get the help of the living.

And when it is made. Will it fetch a fortune? Not at all. To make a fortune out of your machine you must make others, or get them made.

You cannot make them. If you did you would not grow rich, for it would take you years and years to make but a few.

Therefore you get other men to make them, other men to sell them, other men to work them, and get others to buy the cloth they weave, and *you* take the profit.

Do you call that getting rich by your own

unaided industry? I don't. I call it taking a selfish advantage of your own good fortune and the necessity of your fellow creatures.

You will understand that I do not blame you. In a time of competition it behoves every man to look after himself. If I invented a machine I should take the royalty on the patent, and use it as best I might.

But it would be far better for me, and for the world, if I was not compelled to take it ; but might give my talents freely to mankind without danger of being branded as a pauper, or left to die in a ditch as a reward.

You will often hear it said, John, that Socialists are dishonest men, who wish to take the wealth of others and enjoy it themselves. John, that is a lie. It is a wilful, wicked lie, deliberately uttered by robbers who wish to hold fast to the spoil they have taken from the poor.

Socialism is terribly just, implacably honest. It is so honest that I doubt whether you can so much as look at the light of its honesty without blinking ; although you are a fairly honest man, John Smith, as times go. But let me give you an idea of what I consider the very root principle of all Socialism, and of all Democracy.

This is the principle that there is no such thing as personal independence in human affairs. Man is a unit of society, and owes not only all that he possesses, but all that he *is*, to other men.

Yes. Just as no man can have a right to the land, because no man makes the land, so no man has a right to his self, because he did not make that self.

Men are made what they are by two forces : Heredity and environment. That is to say, by " breed " and the conditions of life.

Take a new-born babe—a Shakespeare or a Stevenson—and put it down upon an uninhabited island, and it will perish of hunger.

Set a savage to suckle it, and it will grow up a savage.

Your intellect and character are at birth what your forefathers made them. And the intellects and characters of your forefathers were what their forefathers and their own surroundings made them.

After birth, you become just what your circumstances and the people around you acting upon your peculiar character and intellect, may make you.

Born amongst sots and thieves, and reared amongst them, you will almost certainly become a sot and a thief.

Born and reared amongst Thugs you would have learned and grown to delight in murder.

Whatsoever you are, you are what your forefathers, your circumstances, and your companions have made you. You did not make yourself; therefore you have no right to yourself. You were made by other men; therefore to those other men you are indebted for all you have and for all you are, and Socialism, with its awful justice, tells you that *you must pay the debt.*

Allow me to illustrate this position by using myself as an example. I am a writer. I write a story, and I sell it to the public. Suppose I can, by the sale of many copies, secure a large sum of money. Am I justified in calling that money mine; in asserting, as so many men do assert, that I have earned the money by my own industry and talent, and that therefore it belongs to me alone, by right? I don't know what you think, John Smith, but I *know* that I have not done that work without help, and that in justice I must pay back to *all* men what they have lent me.

What have they lent me? They have lent me all that I have and all that I am.

Who taught me to read, and to write? Who suckled me, nursed me, clothed me, fed me, cured me of my fevers and other ailings?

Where did I get my ideas, my thoughts, my power, such as it is, of literary arrangement, form and style?

I tell you frankly that I don't know. What do I owe to Solomon, to Shakespeare, to Rabelais, to Carlyle, to Dickens; to a hundred other writers? What do I owe to personal friends; to schoolmasters, to the people I have rubbed shoulders and touched hands with all these years? What do I owe to the workshop, to the army, to the people of the inns, the churches, the newspaper offices, the markets, and the slums? I don't know. I can only tell you that these people have made me what I am, and have taught me all I know.

Nay, could I even write a story after all my learning and being and suffering, if I had not fellow creatures to write about? Could I have written "The Ramchunders" if I had not served with soldiers, or "My Sister," if there had been no unfortunate, desperate women in our streets?

All I know, all that even a great writer knows of art or human nature has been learned from other men. Now I tell you, Practical John, that I am in the *debt* of my instructors. Indeed you would see clearly enough that if Mr. Luke Fildes, the artist, engaged a man to sit as a model for his "Casuals," he ought to pay that man his wages. And why should not Charles Dickens pay the models for his article on Tramps?

I owe a debt, then, to the living and the dead. You may say that I cannot pay the dead. But suppose the dead have left heirs! Likely enough they have left heirs. And Socialism, with its awful justice, tells me that the claims of those heirs are binding on me.

Or there may be a *will.* Let us instance a case of this. To none, in my peculiar mental make up, am I more indebted than to Jesus Christ. Well, *he* left a will. His will expressly bids me treat all men as brothers. And to the extent of my indebtedness to Christ am I bound to pay all men, his heirs.

And even after all these debts are considered, I, as the author of a poor little tale, am still in the same position as the inventor of the loom, for I cannot so much as get a copy printed without the aid of myriads of living workmen and of dead inventors.

The pen I write with, the paper I write upon, the types, the press, the engine, the trains, the printer, the carrier, the shopman, even the poor little bare-footed newsboy in the street, are all necessary to *my* "greatness," to *my* "fame," to *my* "wealth." And, after all, suppose no one would *buy* my book or read it! Who does buy it? Who reads it? Men and women I never saw. And who taught them to read? For to those teachers also I owe something.

Now, after all that, John Smith, don't you think I should be a most ungrateful and conceited prig if I had the impudence to hold up my face and say "alone I did it"?

Here is a drawing. It represents a tree by a river. An apple has fallen from the tree, and a monkey wishes to get the apple.

Think of these things, John Smith. They may not strike you as " practical," but they are true.

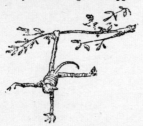

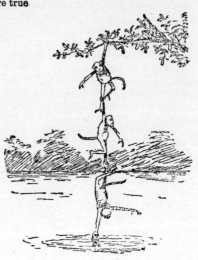

But he cannot reach it. Another monkey tries, but *he* cannot reach it. Then a third monkey comes and plucks the apple out of the water.

Now, John, if that third monkey, who reached the water over the bodies, and by the aid of the other two, were to claim the whole of the apple as his! would you call that *fair?*

It is just as unfair as it is for an author or an inventor to claim fame and fortune as the just reward of "his own industry and talent."

CHAPTER X.

NOW, John Smith, pull yourself together, and remember that you are a practical, hard-headed man. I want to ask you some questions.

Of a country where the idle men were rich, and the industrious men poor, where men were rewarded not for usefulness or goodness, but for successful selfishness, would you not say that its methods were unjust and that its Government was bad?

But of a country where the workers got more than the idlers, and where useful and good men were honoured and rewarded, would you not say that it was a just and well-governed people?

You would. You would call that a false society where the good and the useful suffered, while the bad and the useless prospered.

And you would call that a true society where every man enjoyed the fruits of his own labour, and where the best men were at the head of affairs.

Well, John, we have seen that in this country the greatest share of the wealth goes to those who do nothing to produce it; that industrious men are generally poor, and rich men chiefly idle, the best and the most useful men are not the best paid nor the best rewarded, and that very often the greatest enemies of society reap the most benefit from society's labour.

In short, English society is not a just society, nor is England a well-governed nation.

Now, what is the cause of this? How does it come to pass that Industry and Self-sacrifice are often poor, and that Idleness and Selfishness are often rich? How comes it that laziness and greed reap honour and wealth, whilst poverty and contumely are the lot of diligence and zeal?

By what means do the rich retain their riches; and by what means are the poor deprived of the wealth they create?

There are two causes of this injustice, John. The first is " prerogative," and the second is "competition."

The instrument by means of which our landed aristocrats wrest their riches out of the-hands of the workers is "prerogative," or privilege.

Noblemen have had their estates given to them by the crown—often for some base or cruel deed—and they keep them by means of laws made by a parliament of landlords. The English Parliament of to-day is a Parliament of privilege. It is not a democratic body. Abolish election fees, pay your members, pass acts for granting universal suffrage, second ballot, and one man one vote, and you will have a Parliament elected upon democratic lines. At present there are not a dozen workmen amongst the six hundred and sixty members; and *then* there is the House of Lords.

So much for the great realm of Rent. Outside that we come to the still greater realm of commerce. Here there is not much prerogative, but there is a more deadly thing, there is competition. Competition is the instrument by which, in the commercial world, one man possesses himself of the fruits of other men's labour.

In the world of commerce there are two chief classes. The employers and the employed. Both these classes are engaged in competition. One employer competes against another, and one worker competes against another. The result being that the workers always suffer.

Let us, then, examine these two kinds of competition; and let us examine them as they affect:—

1. The middleman, or employer.
2. The producer, or worker.
3. The consumer, or user.

The rule of trade, throughout the entire commercial world, is that every seller shall obtain as much as he can get for the thing he has to sell, and that every buyer shall give as little as the seller will take for the thing he has to buy.

Suppose I were cultivating a plot of land with a wooden spade, and that with an iron spade I could do as much work in one hour as with a wooden spade I could do in two hours. The value of an iron spade to me would be the amount of labour saved until the spade was worn out.

Now if there were only one iron spade to be bought, it would be worth my while to give for it almost the full amount of the advantage I should gain by its use.

That is to say, if with the iron spade I could raise 20 bushels of wheat in a year, and if with the wooden spade I could only raise 10 bushels of wheat in a year, and if the iron spade would last two years, then I could give 19 bushels of wheat for an iron spade and still gain a bushel a year. So the iron spade would be *worth* to me 19 bushels of wheat.

But now, suppose instead of one iron spade there were a million of iron spades to sell. Would an iron spade be worth less to me? No. It would still do double the work of the wooden spade, and I could only use one iron spade at once. To the buyer the abundance or scarcity of an article makes no difference in its value. A thing bought is worth what it will bring.

On the other hand, what is the value of the spade to the man who makes it? Its value is regulated by the time spent upon making it. If in the time it takes the man to make a spade he could have raised 20 bushels of wheat, then the spade must be sold for 20 bushels of wheat, or he had better give up making spades and stick to his land. But if, in the time it would take him to raise 20 bushels of wheat he can make 10 spades, then to him each spade is only worth 2 bushels of wheat. That is to say that to the seller the abundance of the thing he has to sell does make a difference in its value. A thing sold is worth what it has cost.

Now let us see in what relations this buyer and seller of spades stand to each other as just men, and as traders.

In justice, the day's work of the farmer should be sold for the day's work of the smith. So if a smith can make ten spades whilst a farmer is raising 20 bushels, then the just price of spades is two bushels each.

As traders, it will *pay* me to give 19 bushels of wheat for one iron spade, since that spade will bring me 20 bushels extra.

Therefore, if there is only one smith, and if he will not sell a spade for less than 19 bushels, I shall certainly pay that price.

Under these circumstances the smith will soon grow rich.

But there is my side of the bargain as well as his. I may refuse to pay that price, knowing that he can only buy wheat from me.

In that case he must lower the price of his spades, or dig his own wheat. In the end we should probably come to a fair arrangement.

But suppose there are two men growing wheat, and only one making spades. Then the two farmers are in competition, and the smith may raise the price of his spades.

Or, if there are two smiths and only one farmer, then the price of spades will fall.

Why? Because it will pay the smith better to take three bushels for his spades than to grow wheat; therefore each smith will drop his price, so as to secure the order of the one farmer, down to the point where making spades ceases to pay better than growing wheat.

But, now, suppose that not only are there two smiths, and only one farmer, but that the one farmer owns the whole of the land. Then the smiths are obliged to sell spades or starve, and they will farther drop their prices down to the lowest point at which they can manage to exist.

What does this mean? It means that in the commercial world, where prices are ruled by competition, buyers do not pay for an article the price it is worth to them, but only the price which the seller is in a position to demand.

Let us now consider the effect of competition amongst the workers.

The worker has nothing to sell but his labour, and he must sell that to the middleman. Now suppose a middleman wants a potato patch dug up; and suppose there are two men out of work. Will the middleman pay one of the men a just price, and charge the labour to the consumer of the potatoes? No. He will ask the men what they will do it for, and give the work to the man who will do it at the lower price. Nor is that the end of the mischief.

Say one man gets the work at 3s. a day. The other man is still unemployed. He, therefore, goes to the middleman and offers to do the work for 2s. a day. Then the other man is thrown out of work and must go in for 1s. 6d. a day—or starve.

And so we see that competition amongst the workers reduces the workers' wages, and either increases the middleman's profits or lowers the price of potatoes.

It would pay the workers better to combine.

Then they might force the middleman to pay one of them 5s. a day, which they could share. By this means they would each have 2s. 6d. a day, whereas competition between them would result in one of them working for 1s. 6d a day and the other getting nothing. This is the idea of the trade unionist.

Consider next the effect of competition amongst the middlemen. There are two farmers growing potatoes. Each farmer wishes to get all the trade. Both know that the public will always buy the cheapest article. One farmer drops his price. This *compels* the other to drop his price, for if he did not he would lose all his trade. And when he drops his price the first drops his still lower, and so on, until neither farmer is making any profit. And *then* they compel their men to work for less wages.

And so we see that competition amongst middlemen reduces profits, reduces wages, and cheapens potatoes.

This, of course, applies to all trades and not only to the potato trade.

Now, John, your friends the capitalist members of Parliament, and *their* friends the stupid and dishonest men who farm the newspaper Press, will tell you that wages are regulated by the law of supply and demand, and that it is to the interest of the worker that the prices of all things should be low.

Both these statements are lies.

Wages in this country are not regulated by the law of supply and demand. They are regulated by competition, and it is not to the interest of the workers that commodities should be cheap.

We will now deal with this law of supply and demand.

Many people have got muddled over this law of supply and demand. Their confusion is caused by a failure to understand the difference between natural and artificial cheapness.

Suppose we have a community of two men. One of them grows wheat, the other catches fish, and they exchange their produce.

If the fisherman has a bad catch and gets less fish than usual, then he cannot give so much fish for so much wheat as he is wont to do. That is to say, fish is naturally *dear*. If the farmer has a bad harvest, then wheat is naturally dear. If the fisherman has a great haul of fish, then he can give, perhaps, ten times as many fishes as usual for a loaf of bread. Fish is naturally "cheap." That is to say, it is justly cheap.

But now suppose we have a community of three men. One is a farmer, and claims the land as his. Another is a fisherman who owns the only boat. The third is a labourer who owns nothing but his strength. He cannot grow wheat, for the farmer will not let him use the land, nor catch fish, for the fisherman will not lend him his boat.

He goes then to the farmer as a labourer, for wages ; and the farmer gives him, as wages, just as much wheat as will keep him alive.

The result of this arrangement is that as there are now two men working on the land there will be twice as much wheat.

The farmer now gets two shares of wheat, but as he only pays his labourer half a share and keeps a share and a half for himself he can give more wheat to the fisherman for his fish. That is to say that wheat is now unjustly cheap. It is cheap not because of the bounty of nature, but because the labourer has been swindled out of his rights.

Something of the same kind would happen in a community consisting of one farmer and two fishermen. The two fishermen would want wheat, and would undersell each other. So fish would become cheap to the farmer, not because of the law of supply and demand, but because of competition. That is to say, because of the disorganisation of industry.

One of the most flagrant instances of blundering on this subject was the speech of Mr. Thomas Burt, M.P., when he told the Durham miners they were wrong to strike, because "they might as well try to resist the force of gravity as try to keep up wages in a falling market."

But there must be a demand for coal. Coal is a necessary article, and the consumption is rising yearly. The public want coal. They must have coal. Turn back now to what I said about the exchange of corn for spades. The same rule applies to the purchase of coal. The public will pay for coal up to the limit of its value to them—if they cannot get it at a lower price.

It was not therefore a decrease in the demand for coal which caused the falling market. What was it? It was *competition.*

A few months before the Durham strike one of the Durham firms took a contract for 280,000 tons of coal at 2s. 6d. a ton below the Yorkshire prices.

I said then that the Durham coal owners would try to reduce wages, and so they did.

Their excuse was a "falling market." The market *was* falling. But it was falling because they, in their greedy desire to steal the Yorkshire trade. had lowered their prices.

Take the case of the Cheshire salt trade. There was a falling market there. Salt went a begging. The salt manufacturers made no profits ; the men got low wages. Why? Because one firm kept undercutting another. And I suppose Mr. Burt would have said that it would be as easy to resist the force of gravity as to keep up the price of salt in a falling market.

But when the salt syndicate was formed the market rose. Why? Because all the salt was in the hands of one firm, and there was no competition. So the price of salt went up, and remained up until private firms were formed outside the syndicate and competition began. Then, of course, the price came down.

The history of the Standard Oil Trust in America shows the same thing.

If all the coal mines in England belonged to one man we should hear nothing about falling markets. Coal would rise in price.

Put the mines into the hands of two men. and the prices would come down, because one owner would undersell the other.

The present code of commercial ethics is, in my opinion, opposed entirely to reason and justice. Nearly all our practical economists of to-day put the consumer first, and the producer last. This is wrong. There can be no just or sane system which does not first consider the producer, and then wisely and equitably regulate the distribution of the things produced.

And here is an exposition of the reason and justice of my position. The community is worked by the division of labour. That division of labour ought to be equal and fair. If a collier or a tram-guard is overworked or underpaid, he is being unjustly dealt with by the community whom he serves. Take an illustration. Reduce the complex community to a simple one.

There are one hundred families in a small state. Ten are wood-cutters, ten hunters, ten shoemakers, ten tailors, ten fishermen, and so on. Suppose the wood-cutter works fifteen hours a day, and only receives half as much food and clothing in return as is received by the rest of the community who work ten hours a day. That means that fuel is cheap to ninety families, but that all other things are dear to ten families. It means that ten families are suffering for the advantage of ninety families. It means that the public of that state sweat and swindle the wood-cutters.

In short, wood is unfairly *cheap.*

Take the case of a tram-guard working, say, sixteen hours a day for £1 a week. That man is being robbed of all the pleasure of his life. His wife and children are being deprived of necessary food and comfort. Now there ought to be two guards working eight hours at £2 a week. If the tram company makes big dividends the increased cost should come out of those dividends. If the dividend will not pay it, the fares should be raised. If the public cannot afford to pay bigger fares they ought to walk. At present, supposing the dividends to be low, the public are riding at the expense of the tram-guard's wife and children.

CHAPTER XI.

WE saw just now that competition amongst the workers lowered wages, and that competition amongst the middlemen lowered both wages and profits. We also saw that both kinds of competition lowered the price of goods to the consumer or user.

This is the one great argument in favour of competition—that it reduces the price of commodities or goods.

It is quite true, as I explained before, that we can buy things more cheaply under competition than under a monopoly, and this is urged as sufficient proof that competition is a good thing. "For," say the defenders of the system, "we are all consumers, and what is good for the consumer is good for all."

Now, John, I will prove to you beyond all question that the one argument advanced in favour of competition is really the strongest argument against it.

I will prove to you beyond all question that this much-praised cheapness is not always good for the general consumer, and is never good for the producer—that is to say, for the working class.

First, allow me to expound to you my theory of waste. I call it my theory because I discovered it myself, and because I don't know

that any other writer has ever alluded to it, though I may be wrong in that latter particular. The theory of waste goes to show that excessive cheapness is good for *no one.*

When a thing is *too* cheap we *waste* it. I give you two common examples of this: salt and matches.

Many years ago, whilst riding in a train, I noticed a drunken man wasting matches. I had noticed the same thing before, but had never thought about it. This time I did think about it.

There happened just then to be a good deal of talk going on about the wretched wages and long hours of the match and match-box makers. I began to add things up.

I saw that at one end of the trade we had people working long hours for low wages to make matches; and that at the other end of the trade we had people wasting matches.

Tell me, John Smith, from your own experience, is it not true that of the gross number of matches bought at least one-half are wasted?

I asked myself, firstly, " Why do people waste matches?" The answer was ready— " Because matches are so *cheap.*"

I asked myself, secondly, " Why are match-makers so badly paid?" The answer was longer coming, but it came at last, in the same words, " Because matches are so cheap."

Now, John, I saw plainly enough that when I wasted matches I was really wasting the flesh and blood of the fellow creatures who made them. But I could not see so plainly how that waste might be avoided.

" If," I thought, " the price of matches were doubled, that would pay the match-makers good wages, and it would not hurt me, for I should cease to waste them, and so should only need one box where I now use two."

But then came the question, "Would not that throw half the match-makers out of work; and if it did, what would become of them?"

That question puzzled me for some time; but at last I answered it, and then I began to see all the iniquity of our commercial system, and to understand the causes of the trouble.

A few years later, in an article on the Salt Trade, I said that salt was too cheap, and that the proper remedy was to regulate the price by wages, and not the wages by the price. Thereupon I was attacked by the editor of a northern paper, who denied my statement, and suggested that I was an ass.

This editor said :—

The suggested method of first fixing a good wage for the labour force engaged in production, and afterwards fixing the price for the market of the commodities produced upon the basis of that wage, is chimerical. Take an instance. Blatchford, in his paper, the *Clarion*, a paper devoted to bad economics and music-hall twaddle, instances the Cheshire salt trade. He thinks the "producers" should have their wages fixed at a decent sum, and the price of salt to the public regulated by this item. Suppose it to be attempted, how would it work? It would involve a higher price for salt in the country to begin with. We could afford that. There would be less salt used, and less called for. That would mean there would be fewer men needed to produce salt. *That is, many men employed in that particular industry would be discharged, and would betake themselves to some other congested branch of industry, to overcrowd the workers there, while those that remained would be put on short time! How does this solve the problem?*

Now we can draw two inferences from that statement. The first is, that the only effect of increasing the price of salt would be to throw half the men out of work; the second is, that as those men could find no other employment they had better be left alone.

We will begin with the second statement, and I will show you what nonsense the newspapers of this great country print for your instruction, my practical, hard-headed friend.

To begin with, you see that this editor admits three things, any one of which is sufficient to have shown him that there is something very rotten in our present system of trade.

He owns that if the saltworkers were thrown out of work they could find no means of living because the other branches of industry are "congested.'' That is to say, that men able and willing to work cannot find work in this best of all possible countries.

But he does not tell you why this evil exists, nor how to cure it.

He owns that a great deal of salt is wasted, and that the consumer would be quite as well off if he paid double the price he now pays.

Just consider, John, what these admissions mean. They mean that a useful product of nature is being wasted, and they mean that the labour of a large number of men and women is being wasted, and they mean that both these wastes could be stopped without hurting anyone.

But this intelligent editor will not allow us to interfere, because by stopping the waste we should throw a number of men out of work.

Well, John, what are those men doing? They are wasting their time, and they are wasting salt; but we must let them go on.

Our wise editor acknowledges that the salt they make is being wasted, but yet we are to continue to pay them wages for wasting it. What do you think of him?

His plan is *worse* than that of employing men to dig holes and fill them up again. For *then* they would only waste time. But our clever writer makes them waste salt as well. So that his plan is as foolish as paying men to make salt and throw it into the river. He is one of those stupid people who think it is all right so long as you find the men "employment." It is of no consequence whether their work is useful work or wasteful work, so long as they are kept working. As though a man could eat work, and drink work, and wear work, and put work in the penny bank against a rainy day.

What the people want is food and clothing and shelter and leisure; not *work*. Work is a means, and not an end. Men work to live, they do not live to work.

And the joke of the thing is that if these salt-boilers were out of work, and we suggested that the corporation of their town should employ them to make new roads, or drains, to keep them from starving, this misleader of the people would be the first to sit upon his editorial chair and protest against the employment of the people on "unnecessary work."

Or suppose some Socialist writer turned our editor's argument against the use of machinery, and said that no machinery ought to be introduced, as its effect would be to throw numbers of men out of employment, and drive them to seek work in other industries already congested! What do you think our editor would call that Socialist?

And now, John, allow me to add up the sum in two ways, first as our editor adds it up, and then as I add it up, and see which answer looks most reasonable.

THE EDITOR'S WAY.

Half the domestic salt is wasted. Double the price, and the waste would cease. Then only half as much salt would be bought. Therefore only half as much would be made. Therefore only half the hands would be needed. Therefore half the hands would be out of work.

MY WAY.

Half the domestic salt is wasted. Double the price, and *save half the salt.* Then only half as much would be bought. Therefore only half as much would be made. *Therefore* the salt-makers who now work twelve hours a day, *need only work six hours a day.*

How does that strike you, John? Or you might let them work twelve hours a day, and double their wages. In which case half of them can be sent to do other work. Or you can reduce the hours to eight, and pay them 50 per cent. more wages, in which case a quarter of the men can find other work. The advantages of this plan would be that—

1. No salt is wasted; therefore the supply of salt will last twice as long.

2. The consumer still gets all the salt he can use at the price he paid for salt before.

3. The manufacturer gets the same price for one ton that he used to get for two tons. Therefore he saves enough in carriage, in wear and tear of machinery, in interest on capital, in rent and other ways, to leave him a handsome profit.

4. The worker has only half as much work to do; therefore he secures a six hours' day, and his wages remain as they were.

How does *that* solve the problem?

That, John, is my theory of waste. I call it a practical, hard-headed way of looking at things. What do *you* think?

Just apply the idea to all the trades where labour or material is being wasted, and you will begin to know a great deal more than the average newspaper editor, who gets his salary by wasting ink and paper, and perpetuating follies and lies, will ever find out—unless some sensible person comes to help him.

CHAPTER XII.

BESIDES the theory of waste, we have another aspect of cheapness to consider. The defenders of competition say that competition lowers the price of commodities to the consumer, and they tell us that "as we are all consumers, what is good for the consumer is good for all."

This is not true, John Smith; for though we are all consumers, we are not all producers.

Remember, John, that the consumer is the *user,* and though he is called the "buyer," he is more frequently the "taker."

But the producer is the maker—the worker. The interests of these two classes are not the same. It is the interest of the buyer and the taker that the things made by the worker should be sold cheaply. But it is to the interest of the worker that the things he makes should fetch a high price.

The stupid party will tell you, John, that

since you have many things to buy and only one thing to sell, it is to your interest that all things should be cheap.

That looks plausible. But, John, what *is* the one thing you have to sell? It is your labour. And with the money you get for your labour you have to pay for all you get.

Now cheap goods mean cheap labour, and cheap labour means low wages.

You have nothing but your labour to sell, and you are told that it will pay you to sell that cheaply.

Go to a manufacturer and explain to him that it is to his interest to sell his woollens cheap, and he will call you a fool. Tell a greengrocer that it is to his interest to sell his cabbages cheap, and he will throw one at you. Why, then, my hard-headed friend, do you believe that your interest lies in selling your labour cheap?

You don't believe it. No, what you believe is, that it is to your interest that the men of other trades should sell *their* labour cheap.

But there you may be mistaken. For instance, farm labour is cheap. Hence cheap bread. But hence also the rush of farm-labourers to the towns. Which causes an increase in rent, a decrease in health, and supplies a large bulk of blackleg labour with which the capitalist can defeat you when you strike.

And now let me explain this matter clearly and fully.

In a country where the users were all makers prices would not matter. Suppose you are a weaver, I am a farmer. I give so much corn for so much cloth. If I raise my price you raise yours. That is to say, we simply exchange on equal terms.

But in a country where some of the users are *not* makers, it is to the interest of the makers that prices should be high. Thus:—

You are a weaver, I am a farmer. But you work for a cotton-lord and I for a landlord. We have now four consumers. and only two producers. That is to say, that you and I have now each only one person to buy from; but we have each three people to sell to.

I buy cloth from you, and I sell corn to you, to the landlord, and to the cotton-lord.

You buy corn from me, and sell cloth to me, to the landlord, and the cotton-lord. Thus :—

| Weaver's Customers | { | Landlord. Cotton-lord. Farmer. | Farmer's Customers | { | Landlord. Cotton-lord. Weaver. |

I produce one quarter of wheat and sell it at 40s., of which I pay 20s. in rent. You make one piece of cloth and sell it at 40s., of which your employer takes 20s. in profits. Here is the account :—

One quarter of wheat.... { Rent 20 / Wages 20 } 40

One piece of cloth .... { Profit 20 / Wages 20 } 40

Now when that is sold you will find that each of the four persons gets one quarter. Thus :—

By sale of wheat to Landlord 10
to Cotton-lord .. 10
to Weaver 10
to Self 10
—
40

By sale of cloth to Landlord 10
to Cotton-lord ... 10
to Farmer 10
to Self 10
—
40

Now suppose we raise the price 50 per cent. and see how it works out :—

One quarter of wheat.... { Rent 20 / Wages 40 } 60

One piece of cloth .... { Profit 20 / Wages 40 } 60

And we sell it, as before, each to his three customers and himself :—

By sale of wheat to Landlord 10
to Cotton-lord .. 10
to Weaver 20
to Self 20
—
60

By sale of cloth to Landlord 10
to Cotton-lord ... 10
to Farmer 20
to Self 20
—
60

You will see that the landlord and the cotton lord now only get half as much corn and cloth as we get. How is that?

It is because the price of the goods has been raised, but the rent and interest have not been raised. The two idlers have still the same money to spend, but it will not buy them as much. Whereas at the low prices we, the workers, only got one-half of our earnings, we now get two-thirds of our earnings. Whereas the two idlers got one-half our earnings they now only get one-third of our earnings.

This means that we have doubled our wages. It means that the value of labour has gone up, and that the value of money has gone down.

Before we can go any further, John, I must show you my method of dividing the nation into three classes, instead of into two classes as is usual.

You are used to the common division of the people into two classes, thus :—

    1. The rich idlers.
    2. The poor workers.

And you too often suppose that only the idle rich are useless, and that all the workers are useful.

This is an error. By this division you get a small class of non-producers and a large class of producers.

But if you add to the idle rich all the domestic servants and other people who wait upon them, you will find a large class of non-producers and a larger class of producers.

But then again you must sub-divide this large class of producers into two classes :—

    1. The producers of useful things.
    2. The producers of useless things.

And you will find that a very large number of the workers are really the servants of the rich, and are working at the production of things which only the rich use, and are supported upon the wages which the rich pay them.

Now the rich pay them with the money which they, the rich, get from the class of the producers of necessaries.

A landlord owns an estate and employs two men to cultivate it. We have here only two workers; but we have three eaters. The two men have to keep three.

But if the landlord takes away one of the farmers, and employs him to build the landlord a house, we have then only *one* man producing food, but we have still three men eating it. One man now has to keep three.

You understand me, John? Every person is a consumer of necessaries, and those who produce necessaries have to produce necessaries for all.

Now, the lower the price of necessaries the more necessaries do the rich and his dependents get, and the less do the producers get.

Cheap food and clothing for the producers mean cheap food and clothing for the non-producers.

The non-producers are kept by the rich upon the money taken from the producers.

The cheaper the food and clothing the less do the producers get back from the rich.

The cheaper the food and clothing are the more non-producers can the rich feed.

The more non-producers the rich can feed the more they will withdraw from the work of production.

The more they withdraw from the work of production the fewer there will be to produce food and clothing for all.

The fewer there are to produce food and clothing for all, the harder and the longer must those producers work.

Thus it is quite plain, John, that it is to the interest of the producer that commodities should be dear.

But observe, that it is no use the workers forcing up their wages unless at the same time they can prevent the landlord and the capitalist from raising rent and interest.

As I showed you before, a monopoly can raise prices. But it is well known that a monopoly, like the Oil Trust or Salt Syndicate, while raising prices will not raise wages.

But though a monopoly of capitalists will not serve a useful purpose, it may be possible to find some kind of monopoly that will serve a useful purpose.

What we want is a monopoly which will raise wages and keep down rent and interest. This is to say, a monopoly which will ensure to the worker the enjoyment of all the wealth he produces.

There is only one kind of monopoly which can do this, and it is a *State* monopoly.

Now, a State monopoly is Socialism, and I will proceed to deal with Socialism in my next chapter.

But, before leaving this question of cheapness, I want to anticipate one objection which may be brought against my statement that cheap commodities mean cheap labour.

Some stupid parson, preaching upon a lecture of mine which he had heard, but had not understood, declared that it was nonsense to say that cheap commodities meant cheap labour, for whereas commodities are now universally cheaper than they were, wages are universally higher.

I am not so sure that this is strictly true about the advance in wages and fall in prices. Rents are certainly higher than they were, and meat is dearer. But whether or not it be true that the workers get more money and can buy more with it, that has nothing at all to do with my argument.

All commodities are produced by labour, therefore cheap commodities must result in cheap labour. And you know that as soon as ever prices begin to fall the capitalist begins to talk about lowering wages. And you know that bread and coal and clothing and salt and matches and very many other things are simply cheap because the people who produce them are not half paid.

Matches are so cheap, John, that you can get 800 matches for twopence-halfpenny. Now, John, if the retail price of matches is 2½d. for 800, what is the wholesale price? Put it at twopence.

If the manufacturer charges twopence for 800 matches after allowing for cost of wood, wick, wax, phosphorus, printing, paste, advertisements, carriage, and labour, how much do you suppose the manufacturer pays the women and children who *make* the matches? I don't *know* what these women and children get. I *do* know that I have heard of women and girls working sixteen hours a day for seven days making match boxes, and earning about four shillings a week

by the w rk. And I ask you, How is a woman to live on four shillings a week and pay rent ? And do you ever consider the lives of the people who make these marvellously cheap things ? And do you ever think what kind of homes they have ; in what kind of districts the homes are situated ; and what becomes of those people when they are too ill, or too old, or too infirm to earn even four shillings as the price of · hundred and twelve hours' work?

In my Utopia, when Cain asked, "Am I my brother's keeper," he would be answered with a stern affirmative. In my Utopia a thing would be considered cheap or dear according to the price it *cost*; and not according to the price that was paid for it Matches may be *dear*—from a Utopian point of view—at 2½d. for 800 ; because, you see, it may be necessary to *add* a few items to the cost of production which are *not* charged for in the retail price. As thus :—

Item.—100 women done to death by labour before their time.

Item.—200 children killed by preventible diseases in the slums.

Item.—Say, 10 boys driven into a career of crime by hunger and neglect.

Item.—Say, six girls driven to a life of shame by similar causes.

Item.—The cost of keeping several broken old male and female paupers.

Item.—Pauper graves for the same.

Item.—Cost of fat beadle kept to superintend the above old wrecks.

Item.—An increase of rates for police and prison officials.

Item.—The parish doctor, the dealer in adulterated gin, the scripture reader, the coffin maker, and a fraction of the Cabinet Minister's time spent in proving that "you cannot interfere with the freedom of contract" nor "tamper with the economic balance between producer and consumer."

Add all these items on to the match bill, Mr. Smith, and tell me if you call those matches cheap.

CHAPTER XIII.

JOHN SMITH, do you know what Socialism is? You have heard it denounced many a time, and it is said that you do not believe in it; but do you know what it is ? Good or bad, wise or foolish, it is all I have

to offer as a remedy for the many evils of which I have been complaining. Good or bad, wise or foolish, Socialism is the only remedy in sight. None of its opponents, none of your friends, the members of Parliament, old trade union leaders, Tory and Liberal editors, parsons, priests, lawyers, and men of substance have any remedy to offer at all.

Some of them are sorry, or profess to be sorry, that there is so much misery in the land; some of them offer a little mild charity, some a little feeble legislation, but there is no great radical cure to be heard of except Socialism.

What is Socialism? I am going to tell you, and I ask you to listen patiently, and to judge fairly. You have heard Socialism reviled by speakers and writers. You know that the Pope has denounced it, and that the Bishop of Manchester has denounced it. You know that men like Herbert Spencer, Charles Bradlaugh, and John Morley have written and spoken against it, and doubtless you have got an idea that it is as unworthy, as unwise, and as unworkable as such men say it is. Now, I will describe it for you and you shall draw your own conclusions.

But before I tell you what Socialism is, I must tell you what Socialism is not. For half our time as champions of Socialism is wasted in denials of false descriptions of Socialism; and to a large extent the anger, the ridicule, and the argument of the opponents of Socialism are hurled against a Socialism which has no existence except in their own heated minds.

Socialism, John, does not consist in violently seizing upon the property of the rich and sharing it out amongst the poor. Socialists do not propose by a single act of Parliament, or by a sudden revolution, to put all men on an equality, and compel them to remain so. Socialism is not a wild dream of a happy land where the apples will drop off the trees into our open mouths, the fish come out of the rivers and fry themselves for dinner, and the looms turn out ready-made suits of velvet with golden buttons without the trouble of coaling the engine. Neither is it a dream of a nation of stained-glass angels, who never say damn, who always love their neighbours better than themselves, and who never need to work unless they wish to.

No, Mr. Smith, Socialism is none of those things. It is a scientific scheme of national Government, entirely wise, just and *practical*. And now let us see.

For convenience sake Socialism is generally divided into two kinds. These are called—

1. Practical Socialism.
2. Ideal Socialism.

Really they are only part of one whole; Practical Socialism being a kind of preliminary step towards Ideal Socialism, so that we might with more reason call them Elementary and Advanced Socialism.

I am an Ideal Socialist, and desire to have the whole Socialistic programme carried out.

Practical Socialism is so simple that a child may understand it. It is a kind of national scheme of co-operation, managed by the State. Its programme consists, essentially, of one demand, that the land and other instruments of production shall be the common property of the people, and shall be used and governed by the people for the people.

Make the land and all the instruments of production State property; put all farms, mines, mills, ships, railways, and shops under State control, as you have already put the postal and telegraphic services under State control, and Practical Socialism is accomplished.

The postal and telegraphic service is the standing proof of the capacity of the State to manage the public business with economy and success.

That which has been done with the post-offices may be done with mines, trams, railways, and factories.

The difference between Socialism and the state of things now in existence will now be plain to you.

At present the land—that is, England—does not belong to the people—to the English—but to a few rich men. The mines, mills, ships, shops, canals, railways, houses, docks, harbours, and machinery do not belong to the people, but to a few rich men.

Therefore the land, the factories, the railways, ships, and machinery are not used for the general good of the people, but are used to make wealth for the few rich men who own them.

Socialists say that this arrangement is unjust and unwise, that it entails waste as well as misery, and that it would be better for all, even for the rich, that the land and other instruments of production should become the property of the State, just as the post-office and the telegraphs have become the property of the State.

Socialists demand that the State shall manage the railways and the mines and the mills just as it now manages the post-office and the telegraphs.

Socialists declare that if it is wicked and foolish and impossible for the State to manage the factories, mines, and railways, then it is wicked and foolish and impossible for the State to manage the telegraphs.

Socialists declare that as the State carries the people's letters and telegrams more cheaply and more efficiently than they were carried by private enterprise, so it could grow corn and weave cloth and work the railway systems more cheaply and more efficiently than they are now worked by private enterprise.

Socialists declare that as our Government now makes food and clothing and arms and accoutrements for the army and navy and police, so it could make them for the people.

Socialists declare that as many corporations make gas, provide and manage the water-supply, look after the paving and lighting and cleansing of the streets, and often do a good deal of building and farming, so there is no reason why they should not get coal, and spin yarn, and make boots, and bread, and beer for the people.

Socialists point out that if all the industries of the nation were put under State control, all the profit, which now goes into the hands of a few idle men, would go into the coffers of the State—which means that the people would enjoy the benefits of all the wealth they create.

This, then, is the basis of Socialism, that England should be owned by the English, and managed for the benefit of the English, instead of being owned by a few rich idlers, and mismanaged by them for the benefit of themselves.

But Socialism means more than the mere transference of the wealth of the nation to the nation.

Socialism would not endure competition. Where it found two factories engaged in under-cutting each other at the price of long hours and low wages to the workers it would step in and fuse the two concerns into one,

save an immense sum in cost of working, and finally produce more goods and better goods at a lower figure than were produced before.

But Practical Socialism would do more than that. It would educate the people. It would provide cheap and pure food. It would extend and elevate the means of study and amusement. It would foster literature and science and art. It would encourage and reward genius and industry. It would abolish sweating and jerry work. It would demolish the slums and erect good and handsome dwellings. It would compel all men to do some kind of useful work. It would recreate and nourish the craftsman's pride in his craft. It would protect women and children. It would raise the standard of health and morality; and it would take the sting out of pauperism by paying pensions to honest workers no longer able to work.

Why nationalise the land and instruments of production? To save waste; to save panics; to avert trade depressions, famines, strikes, and congestion of industrial centres; and to prevent greedy and unscrupulous sharpers from enriching themselves at the cost of the national health and prosperity. In short, to replace anarchy and war by law and order. To keep the wolves out of the fold, to tend and fertilise the field of labour instead of allowing the wheat to be strangled by the tares, and to regulate wisely the distribution of the seed-corn of industry so that it might no longer be scattered broadcast—some falling on rocks and some being eaten up by the birds of the air.

I will now give you one example of the difference between Socialism and the existing system.

You remember my chapter on Salt and Waste. Under existing conditions what was the state of the salt trade?

The mines and manufacture owned and carried on by a number of firms, each of which competes against all the rest.

Result: Most of the small firms ruined; most of the large firms on the verge of ruin. Salt-boilers, the workmen, working twelve hours a day for 3s., and the public wasting more salt than they use.

Put this trade under State control. They will cease to make salt to waste; they will tablish a six-hours day, and they will raise the wages of the men to, say, two pounds a week.

To pay these extra wages they will abolish all the unnecessary middlemen and go-betweens. The whole industry will be placed under one management. A vast number of clerks, agents, travellers, canvassers, and advertisers will be dispensed with, the salaries of the managers will be almost entirely saved, and the cost of distribution will be cut down by fully seventy-five per cent.

The same system would be pursued with other industries. Take the soap trade. There is one firm which spends over £100,000 a year in advertisement, and the head of that firm makes £100,000 a year in profits. Socialism would save all that advertisement, and would pay a manager a reasonable salary and produce the soap at less than its present cost, whilst paying the workers good wages for shorter hours than they now work.

You will observe that under Practical Socialism there would be wages paid; and, probably, the wages of managers would be higher than the wages of workmen; and the wages of artists, doctors, and other clever and highly-trained men would be higher than those of weavers or navvies.

Under Ideal Socialism there would be no money at all, and no wages. The industry of the country would be organised and managed by the State, much as the post-office now is ; goods of all kinds would be produced and distributed for use, and not for sale, in such quantities as were needed, the hours of labour would be fixed, and every citizen would take what he or she desired from the common stock. Food, clothing, lodging, fuel, transit, amusements, and all other things would be absolutely free, and the only difference between a prime minister and a collier would be the difference of rank and occupation.

I have now given you a clear idea of what Socialism is. If I wrote another hundred pages I could tell you no more. But two important tasks remain for me to do.

First, to give you some idea of the means by which I think Socialism could be established.

Second, to answer the chief arguments commonly used against Socialism by its opponents.

What we have to find out, Mr. Smith, is can Socialism be established, and how?

And is Socialism just and desirable; and practicable if we can succeed in getting it ?

CHAPTER XIV.

THE question is, how can Socialism be accomplished? I confess that I approach this question with great reluctance. The establishment and organisation of a Socialistic State are the two branches of the work to which I have given least attention. Hitherto I have devoted my efforts to teaching the principles of Socialism, and to disproving the arguments brought against it. But I will do my best, merely observing that I can lay claim to no special knowledge, nor to any special aptitude for such a task.

I have no "system" ready cut and dried. I don't think any sensible Socialist would offer such a system. Socialists are practical people in these days, and know that coats must be cut according to cloth.

But on one point I am quite certain, and

that is that the first thing to do is to educate the people in Socialism. Let us once get the people to understand and desire Socialism, and I am sure we may very safely leave them to secure it.

The most useful work which Socialists can do at present is the work of education and organisation.

Socialism will not come by means of a sudden *coup*. It will grow up naturally out of our surroundings, and will develop naturally and by degrees. But its growth and its development may be materially hastened.

It always amuses me to hear the intensely practical person demand, How are you going to do it? When will you make a start? Where do you propose to leave off?

My dear Mr. Smith, it is too late to ask

when we are going to begin. We *have* begun. We, or rather they, began long ago. Nearly all law is more or less Socialistic, for nearly all law implies the right of the State to control individuals for the benefit of the nation. But of late years the law has been steadily becoming more and more Socialistic. I will give you a few examples.

The abolition of toll bars and bridge tolls was Socialistic action, for it made the roads and bridges common property.

Most of the Building Acts, by virtue of which streets must be of a specified width, back-to-back houses are forbidden, &c., are Socialistic, for they take away from the property owner the power to do as he likes with his own.

The Truck Acts are Socialistic, for they deny the employer the power to swindle his workmen.

The Factory Acts are Socialistic, for they deny the employer the power to work women and children to death.

The Compulsory and Free Education Acts are Socialistic. The Acts which compel the inspection of mines and factories, the inspection of boilers, the placing of a load-line on ships, and the granting of relief to paupers, are all Socialistic Acts, for they all interfere with the "freedom of contract" and the "rights of the individual." Finally, the acquirement of the postal and telegraphic arrangements by the State, and the establishment of corporate gas and water works are Socialistic measures, for they recognise the Socialistic principle of common ownership, production, and distribution.

You will see, then, John, that Socialism has begun, so that the question of where to begin is quite superfluous.

As for the question of where we shall leave off, that is a foolish question, and only a fool would try to answer it. There is no such thing as finality. The world will go on after we are dead and forgotten. How do I know what our grandchildren will do? Should I not be a conceited ass to attempt to lay down laws for them? My only duty towards posterity, Mr. Smith, is to smooth the road for them as much as possible, and so give them a fairer chance than we have had to make the best of life.

Socialism will come, John, of that I feel sure. And it will come by paths not seen by me, and will develop in ways which I do not dream of. My task is to help its arrival.

Still, I will offer you, in all modesty, a few ideas on the subject. I can at least point out to you some of the things that need to be done, and I may even suggest what seem to me reasonable ways of doing them.

What are the things to be done? We want to find work for the unemployed. We want to get pensions for the aged. We want to abolish the poor-law system. We want to produce our own food so as to be independent of foreign nations. We want to get rid of the slums and build good houses for the workers. We want to abolish the sweater and shorten hours of labour and raise wages. We want to get rid of the smoke nuisance, and the pollution of rivers; and we want to place the land and all other instruments of production under the control of the State.

Before we can accomplish any of these reforms we must have a public in favour of them, and a Parliament that will give effect to the Popular demands. So that the first thing we need is education, and the second thing we need is a Socialist Party.

I am well aware, John, that you may have a democratic parliament and not get Socialistic measures passed. We see that in America. But if the Democratic Parliament has a Socialistic Public behind it there need be no fear of failure.

Suppose then that we have a Socialistic Public and Parliament. What is to be done? It would be presumption for me to instruct such a Parliament. I am only giving you, John Smith, my poor ideas.

Perhaps we should begin with the land. Perhaps with the unemployed. Perhaps with the mines and railways.

Suppose we began with the land. The land must be made the property of the nation. Very well, what about compensation?

Personally I am against compensation, but I suppose it would have to be given, and my only hope is that it would be kept as low as possible. So with the mines and the railways. They could be bought, and the smaller the price the better.

Then as to the unemployed. They must be registered in their various trades, and set to work.

I should divide them into three principal classes—

1. Agricultural labourers;
2. General labourers;
3. Building trades.

The first I should send to work on State farms, the second to work at public improvements, and the third to build dwelling-houses for the people.

I daresay, John, you will feel rather uneasy at these suggestions, and imagine that I am going to ruin the nation by saddling upon it the keep of a vast army of paupers.

But, my practical friend, the worst use you can put a man to is to make a tramp of him. All the tramps, bear in mind, and all the able-bodied paupers have to be fed and lodged now in some fashion. And although they are badly fed and treated worse than dogs, you must not suppose that they cost little. For you must know that it costs about ninepence to give a pauper threepennyworth of food, and when you take into account the large numbers of policemen and other officials who are paid to watch and punish and attend to the tramps, it will be quite clear that a tramp is a more costly luxury than he appears to be.

But besides that, John, it is much better that a tramp should be making something than marring himself; and you must not suppose that the State farms would be a burden to you. Decently managed they would soon prove a great benefit.

For don't you see, John, that all those hands which are now idle would then be producing wealth, and when I remind you that the best authorities agree that a four hours day would enable the people to produce enough for all, you will see that our unemployed could, on those State farms, very easily keep themselves.

Each of these farms, John, would be the base for the formation of a new communal town—one of the Towns of Merrie England. To it would be sent all kinds of craftsmen: tailors, shoemakers, joiners, and the like, so that each commune would be complete in itself.

Houses, upon a new model, to be arranged by a special State Board of architects, artists, sanitary engineers, and Socialists, would be built for the workers, with baths, libraries, dining-rooms, theatres, meeting-rooms, gardens, and every kind of institution needful for the education, health, and pleasure of the people.

Understand, further, that these men would not be treated as paupers. They would be treated as honourable citizens, and, after rent and other charges had been paid to the State, they would receive all the produce of their labour.

Meanwhile, pensions would be granted to the aged poor, and all the workhouses and casual wards would be abolished.

There would be no such thing as a pauper, or a man out of work, or a beggar or a tramp in all England.

Meanwhile, John, it would be a wise thing to form a commission of the cleverest mechanical engineers and inventors in England for the purpose of developing electricity, so as to do away with steam power, with gas-lighting, and the smoke nuisance.

Then we should, very probably, establish a universal eight hours day, and a plan for educating and feeding all children free at the public schools.

We should nationalise the railways, ships, canals, dock-yards, mines, and farms, and put all those industries under State control.

We should have an Agricultural Minister just as we now have a Postmaster-General. He would be held responsible that the department under him produced bread and vegetables, meat and fruit for 36 millions of people, just as the Postmaster-General is now held responsible for the carriage and delivery of our letters.

So by degrees we should get all the land and instruments of production into the hands of the State, and so by degrees we should get our industry organised. These, John, are my ideas. They are very crude, and of course very imperfect. But don't trouble on that score. When your Public understands Socialism and desires to establish it, there will be no difficulty about plans. Just get a number of your cleverest organisers and administrators into committee and let them formulate a scheme. Depend upon it they will produce a much better scheme than mine, though I think even mine is better than none at all, and, as I said before, I only offer it to give you an idea of the possibilities of the task before us.

CHAPTER XV.

WE will now proceed, Mr. Smith, to consider some of the stock arguments used against Socialism.

Non-Socialists are in the habit of saying that Socialism demands a complete change in human nature. They say Socialism is very pretty in theory, but that it is wrong because human nature is not good enough for Socialism. They tell us that we Socialists are mistaken because we have built up a scheme without first considering human nature. They are entirely mistaken.

The fact is that we Socialists have studied human nature, and that our opponents only object to Socialism because they do not understand human nature at all.

"Socialism," say these critics, "is impossible, because it would destroy the incentive of gain." The incentive of *gain*.

And then they quote the dogma of the political economist :—

The social affections are accidental and disturbing elements in human nature, but avarice *and the desire of progress* are constant elements.

Avarice, they say, is a constant element of human nature, and they proceed to build up what they foolishly call "a science" of human affairs upon this one single element.

They ignore the second element, "The desire of *progress*," which I have marked in italics, and the only conclusion we can come to, after reading their stupid books and shallow articles, is the conclusion that they recognise avarice, that is love of money, as the ruling passion of mankind.

Now this assumption of the economists, Mr. Smith, is due to ignorance, to the densest ignorance of the human nature which they tell us we have failed to study.

Political economy is a science of human affairs. Every science which professes to be a science of human affairs, must be built upon an estimate of human nature. If it is built upon a false conception of human nature, the science is a failure. If it is built upon a true conception of human nature, the science is a success.

Now the political economy of our opponents is built upon a false conception of human nature. In the first place it recognises only one motive, which is sheer folly. In the second place it assumes that the strongest motive is avarice, which is untrue.

These flaws are due to the fact that the founders and upholders of this system of grab and greed are men who have never possessed either the capacity or the opportunity for studying human nature.

Mere book-men, school-men, business-men, and logic-choppers can never be authorities on human nature. The great authorities on human nature are the poets, the novelists, the artists, and the men whose lives and labours bring them into daily contact with their fellow creatures.

The only school for the study of human nature is the world. The only text books are the works of men like Shakespeare, Hugo, Cervantes, Sterne, and other students who learned in that school.

But the effectual study of human nature demands from the student a vast fund of love and sympathy. You will never get admitted into the heart of a fellow-creature unless you go as a friend.

I remember as a child reading a fairy tale of a prince who had given to him a feather of magic properties. When he touched people with that feather they spoke what was in their mind. Such a feather with such powers you may have any day if you will, and the name of it is love. That is the magic feather of Shakespeare, of Sterne, and of Cervantes. If you would witness the manifestation of its power, go to your books and make acquaintance with Sancho Panza and Uncle Toby, and with Rosalind and Dogberry, and Mercutio and Macbeth.

The study of human nature is a most difficult one. Only specially-gifted men can master it ; and that with much pains. Judge then for yourself whether the motley mob of ready-writers in the press are authorities on such a subject. Judge for yourself whether a man who spends all his days in the study of economics and the mathematic sciences is qualified to build up a system which depends upon a deep and wide knowledge of the souls of men. Go now and contrast the Frankenstein monster of the political-economist with Sterne's "Muleteer," Eliot's "Silas Marner," Shakespeare's "Hamlet," or Rabelais' "Panurge," and decide for yourself as to whether or not the study of literature is of any use in the study of Social Science.

Consider the lady nurse at the seat of war. Gentle, delicate, loving, and loveable, of high intelligence, of great beauty, young, refined and educated, she leaves pleasure and home and ease, and all the pomps and flatteries of courts and assemblies, to labour amid peril and hardship and all the sickening and dreadful sounds and sights of the battle-field, the hospital, and the camp. Amid pestilence and blood, amid death and mutilation, you find her, calm and gentle and fearless. Dressing loathsome wounds, soothing fevered heads, hearing the imprecations and the groans of delirious and sick men, always unselfish, always patient, always kind, with but one motive and that charity, without any crown or recompense of glory or reward—such is the lady nurse at the seat of war. It is a noble picture—is it not? Well, *that* is human nature.

Consider now the outcast Jezebel of the London pavement. Fierce and cunning, and false and vile. Ghastly of visage under her paint and grease. A creature debased below the level of the brutes, with the hate of a devil in her soul and the fire of Hell in her eyes. Lewd of gesture, strident of voice, wanton of gaze; using language so foul as to shock the pot-house ruffian, and laughter whose sound makes the blood run cold. A dreadful spectre. shameless, heartless, reckless, and horrible. A creature whose touch is contamination, whose words burn like a flame, whose leers and ogles make the soul sick. A creature living in drunkenness and filth. A moral blight. A beast of prey who has cast down many wounded, whose victims fill the lunatic ward and the morgue: a thief, a liar, a hopeless, lost, degraded wretch, of whom it has been well said, "Her feet take hold of Hell; her house

is the way to the grave, going down to the chamber of death." It is an awful picture—is it not? But *that* is human nature.

There is the character of Don Quixote, *that* is human nature, so is the character of Sancho Panza. The same applies to the characters of Sam Weller and Bill Sikes, of Hermione and Lady Macbeth, of Ancient Pistol and Coriolanus, of Corporal Trim and Corporal Brock, of John Knox and Charles II., of Voltaire and Martin Luther, of Grace Darling and Carmen, of John Wesley and Tom Sayers.

There is human nature in Raleigh's spreading of the cloak before the Queen; in the wounded Sydney giving up the cup of water to the wounded soldier; in Nelson on the deck of the "Victory" with his breast ablaze with orders; in Napoleon afraid to die at Sedan; in St. Paul's endurance of stripes and contumely; in Judas selling his master for thirty pieces of silver.

Human nature is a complex and an awful thing. It is true of man that he is fearfully and wonderfully made. But consider all these types of humanity, picture to yourself the soldier at his post, the thief at his work, the smith at the forge, the factory girl at the loom, the actor on the stage, the priest at his prayers, the sot at his can, the mother with her babe, the widow at the husband's grave, the judge in his wig, the Indian in his paint, the farmer at the plough, the beggar asleep in the ditch, the peer with his betting book, the surgeon with his knife, the street arab in the slums, and the young girl dreaming over a love tale, and then recall to your mind the bloodless, soulless abortion of the political economist, the "unit" of "Society," whose purpose in life is to "produce," and whose only motive power is the "desire for gain."

The last refuge of Gradgrind, when he is beaten by Socialistic argument, is the assertion that human nature is incapable of good. But this is not true. Men instinctively prefer light to darkness, love to hate, and good to evil.

The most selfish man would not see a fellow-creature die or suffer if he could save him without personal cost or risk.

Only a lunatic would wantonly destroy a harvest or poison a well, unless he might thereby reap some personal advantage.

It is clear, therefore, that men will do good for its *own* sake; but they will not do evil except with the hope of gain. And this may be said of the lowest and the basest types of mankind. But of the highest, even of the intermediate types of mankind, how much more may be said? So much more, indeed, as may overthrow Gradgrind and his brutal theories, and bury him and them in the ruins of his arguments of ashes and of his defences of clay. For mankind turn to the sun, even to seeking it through fog and storm. They will obey God's commandment when they can hear it, and resist the temptations of Satan with such power as they possess. True are the words of Tennyson:—

We needs must love the highest when we see it,
Not Launcelot, nor another.

"Miserabler theory"—says Carlyle—"miserabler theory than that of money on the ledger being the primary rule for empires, or for any higher entity than city owls, and their mice-catching, cannot be propounded."

Major Burke, of the Wild West, told me one day that on the prairies the cowboys went about finger on trigger, ever on the *qui vive* for an ambush. If a leaf stirred they fired, if a twig snapped they fired; and in about five cases out of a hundred they shot an Indian.

This is the state in which men live under a competitive commercial system. It is war. The hand of every man is against every man's hand. Men move finger on trigger, and fire at the falling of a leaf. But in a Socialistic state of society they would no more go armed and in fear of their fellow-creatures than did the Wild West Cowboys in London.

Then the Church speaks, saying that men are born bad. Now, I hold that human nature is not innately bad. I take the scientists' view that man is an undeveloped creature. That he is a being risen from lower forms of life, that he is slowly working out his development—in an *upward* direction—and that he is yet a long way from the summit. How far he is below the angels, how far above the brutes, in his pilgrimage is a matter for dispute. I believe that he is a great deal better than the Church and the economist suppose him to be; and that the greater part of what these superior persons call his "badness" is due to the conditions under which he lives, or in which he and his fathers have been bred.

It is no use arguing whether or not man is bad by nature, and without respect to circumstances. Man is a creature of circumstances. You cannot separate him from his surroundings, or he ceases to exist. We will waive the discussion of what man might be, and concede to our opponents the advantage of considering him as he is. We will consider man as we see him, and his circumstances as we see them.

The question asked is whether human nature is bad. We must begin by asking under what circumstances? Will a peach tree bear peaches? Yes, if planted in good soil and against a south wall. Will a rose tree flourish in England? Not if you set it in an ash-heap and exclude the light and air. Is a river a beautiful and a wholesome thing? Yes, when it is fed by the mountain streams, washed by the autumn rains, and runs over a pebbly bed, between grassy meadows, decked with water lilies, fringed with flowering rushes, shaded by stately trees; but not when it is polluted by city sewers, stained by the refuse of filthy dye vats and chemical works; not when its bed is slime, its banks ashes, and when the light falling upon it is the flame of forges, and the shadows those of mills, and manure works, and prisons. Is human nature sweet, and holy, and fruitful of good things? Yes. When it gets light and air and culture, such as we give to the beasts of the farm and to the lilies of the field; but when it is poisoned and perverted and defiled, when it is crushed, cursed, and spat upon, then human nature becomes bad. Tell me, then, shall we, in judging rivers, take the Irwell; or shall we, in judging men, take the slums, or the City Council, or the House of Commons, or the Bourse, or the Stock Exchange, or any other body where vulgarity, and aggression, and rascality, and selfish presumption are the elements of success? No thing on this earth can be good under adverse conditions—not the river, not the green grass, not the skylark, nor the rose. But if a thing can be good under propitious circumstances, we say of it, "This is good." We say that of all the things of the earth except man. Of man we say, without hesitation and without conditions—"He is bad."

We will leave the Mongolian, the Turanian, and other inferior races out of our calculation, and take the Caucasian race as the type of humanity. Then it may be said that several intellectual qualities are common to all men. The average man, under average conditions, is fond of woman, fond of children—especially his own. He is also fond of himself. He likes to succeed. He likes to be admired. He enjoys his food and drink. He likes excitement and variety. He likes to laugh. He admires beauty, and is pleased with music.

Now consider how these qualities of the body and the mind may be acted upon by circumstances. We know how the pure passion of love may be debased. We know how men may become so brutalised that they will ill-use women; that they will cease to love and cherish their children. We know how a man grows selfish and cruel. We know how he sinks to sottishness, to gluttony, to torpid, savage boorishness. We know we have with us vast numbers of rich and poor, of respectable and disreputable liars and rogues and beasts and dastards. Is that the fault of human nature? Or is it the fault of the evil influences that choke and poison human nature?

Gradgrind tells me that greed is the chief motor of the human heart. It has been so called by generations of shallow cynics and stupid dunces before him; and, as he never thinks for himself, he has never found out the error. But let any man look about him and think of what he sees, and I believe that he will agree with me that what phrenologists call " Love of approbation " is a hundred-fold a stronger force than greed. What observer of life will deny this? Is it not plain to all when the eyes are opened that the desire to get praise or admiration is a stronger motive than the desire to get money? Nay, this desire to get wealth is only one out of a thousand consequences of the love of approbation. Only a miser loves money for its own sake. The great bulk of our graspers and grubbers value money for what it will bring. A few, and to a small extent, because it brings them luxury, ease, indulgence. A larger number, and to a greater extent, because it saves them and theirs from the risks of penury

and degradation. A great preponderance, and to the widest extent, because it wins them the admiration, the wonder, the envy, and the services of their fellows.

Greed is *not* the strongest passion of the human heart. A much stronger passion is vanity. Yet I will not say that vanity is the chief motor of human action. Is it too harsh a word—" vanity"? Perhaps it is—in some cases. Or perhaps it only sounds too harsh because often enough vanity is intertwined with other and nobler feelings. One would not call Nelson vain. He had a strong desire to win the love and admiration of his countrymen, no doubt. But twisted in with the threads of that feeling were the golden strands of patriotism, of courage, of duty. We cannot say how much of a hero's life is prompted by his wish to be loved by his countrymen, and how much by his own love *for* his countrymen. I am inclined to think that wherever the desire for approbation can be disentangled from other feelings it may be fairly written down as vanity.

And how far-stretched this vanity is—this love of approbation. From the Prime Minister, airing his eloquence on the integrity of the Empire, or polishing up his flimsy epigrams in his study, down through all the steps of the social ladder—the ambassador in his garter, the general in his plumed hat, the actor in his best part, and the costermonger with pearl buttons on his trousers—all are tinged with vanity, all have in them the desire, the yearning, to be thought well of. This desire is stronger than the thirst for pelf. Men who would scorn to be paid will not scorn to be applauded. It is so strong that *no* man nor woman is free from its influence. Indeed it must be of this importance, for divested of the love and respect of all our fellow creatures, life would cease to be endurable. But life is quite endurable without wealth. And there are many people who do not desire wealth.

Do you think the whole of the prosperous and wealthy classes would resolutely oppose Socialism if they understood it? I don't know about that. Do men seek or hold wealth for its own sake, or for what it will buy? For what it will buy. And the things they suppose they can buy with wealth, what are they? Admiration and enjoyment. Now if you could convince men that admiration and enjoyment could *not* be bought with wealth, but *could* be got without wealth, is it not possible that Mammon would lose his worshippers?

As society is at present constituted, nearly every man gets as much money as he can. What are the ordinary motives for this conduct? Plutocrat says, "I can make a fortune out of the cotton trade, and why should I not? If I don't make it some other man will; and perhaps the other man will be a rogue." You see, men cannot trust each other. Under the operation of unfettered individual enterprise, life is a scramble. A man knows he could live on less than ten thousand a year, and he knows that multitudes are hungry. But if he foregoes the making of a fortune, it will not benefit the poor. Some other man will seize on what he relinquishes, and the scramble will go on. So men amass wealth because they think they might as well do it as let another do it in their stead.

There is another thing. Plutocrat will tell you he has a wife and family to provide for. He knows the world too well to leave a widow and children to the tender mercies of his brother graspers. It is every man for himself, and the weakest to the wall. So he will grind other people to make money to prevent other people from grinding his children. He is right in a great measure. It is his duty to provide for his wife and children; and under our present system of robbery and murder by individual enterprise the widow and the orphan will find none to pity or defend them—unless they can pay for value received.

There is another thing. In a commercial era and in a commercial nation wealth is the reward of merit, the crown of honour, and the sign of virtue. Every Englishman dreads failure. Wealth stamps him with the hall-mark of success, and truly that hall-mark is borne by some very spurious metals; some most evident Brummagem jewels.

It seems, then, that to deprive money grubbing of its power to mislead we must make great social changes. We must assure men that in *no* case should their children want. We must assure men that the possession of wealth will not bring them honour. We must assure men that justice will win them respect and not contempt, and that the good man who forbears to fill his coffers at the public expense need not fear to see some rascal render his generosity abortive.

The Gradgrind supposes greed to be the ruling passion because in the Society he knows most men strive to get money. But *why* do they strive to get money? There are two chief motives. One the desire to provide for or confer happiness upon children or friends; the other the desire to purchase applause. But in the first case the motive is not greed, but love; and in the second case it is not greed, but vanity. Only a *miser* covets money for its own sake. Both love and vanity are stronger passions than greed.

Will the desire of gain make progress? Suppose a man to have a thirst for money and success, but no genius. Can he for a prize of ten thousand pounds invent a printing press? No. For though the impetus is there the genius is absent. But suppose he has the genius and no prize is offered! Can he then invent the machine? Yes. Because he has the genius to do it. We see then that greed cannot invent machines, but genius can.

Now, if a prize be offered for a new machine, will a man of no genius make it? No. He will try, for the sake of the prize; but he will fail for lack of brains. But no prize being offered, will the man of genius, seeing a use for a new machine, invent it? He will. History proves that he *will* invent and *does* invent it, not only without hope of gain, but even at risk of life and liberty.

It seems, then, that genius without mercenary incentives will serve the world; but that mercenary motives without genius will not.

In proof of which argument look back upon the lives of such men as Galileo, Bruno, Newton, and indeed the bulk of the explorers, scientists, philosophers, and martyrs. Love of truth, love of knowledge, love of art, love of fame are *all* stronger motives than the love of gain, which is the *only* human motive recognised by a system of political economy supposed to be founded on human nature.

It is the mistake of a blockhead to suppose that because sometimes genius can make money therefore money can always make genius.

For the sake of love, for the sake of duty, for the sake of pity, for the sake of religion, and for the sake of truth, men and women have resigned their bodies to the flames, have laid their heads upon the block, have suffered imprisonment, disgrace, and torture and starvation. Who will do as much for *money*?

Money never had a martyr. In Mammon's bible the text of the Christian bible is altered. It reads, "What shall it profit a man if he gain the whole world and lose his own life?" Men will *fight* for money; but they will not die for it. Now millions have died for honour, for love, for religion, for duty, for country, for *fame*. And how then can any sensible person stand by the base and brutish dogma that *greed* is the chief motor of the human heart?

It seems an amazing thing to me, this persistence in the belief that greed is the motive power of humanity. The refutation of that error is forever under our noses. You see how men strive at cricket; you see the intense effort and the fierce zeal which they display at football; you see men nearly kill themselves in boat races, on cycling tracks and running grounds; you *know* that these men do all this without the hope of a single penny of gain, and yet you tell men in the face of the powerful football combinations, and rowing clubs, and cricket clubs, and with a quarter of a million of volunteers amongst you, and with the records of Inkerman, and Lucknow, and Marston Moor on your shelves, and with the walls of the hospitals, and the lifeboats of the Royal Humane Society, and the spires of your churches, and the convents of the Sisters of Charity, and the statues of your Cromwells, and Wellingtons, and Nelsons, and Cobdens all ready for you to knock your stupid heads against, that the only reliable human motive is—the desire for gain.

Look about you and see what men do for gain, and what for honour. Your volunteer force—does that exist for gain? Your lifeboat service, again—is *that* worked by the incentive of dirty dross? What will not a soldier do for a tiny bronze cross, not worth a crown piece? What will a husband endure for his wife's sake? a father for his children? a fanatic for his religion? But you do not believe that Socialism is to destroy all love, and all honour, and all duty and devotion, do you?

And now I have addressed you in a homely, simple fashion, allow me to quote a passage or two from Carlyle, and note how he in his magnificent language, and with lavish wealth of dazzling pictures, says what I have said in my weaker and cruder way. Maybe, if you do not think my words of weight, nor my name of force sufficient, you will respect the utterances of one of the greatest thinkers and speakers England ever bred. I quote from "Past and Present":—

Let the captains of industry retire into their own hearts and ask solemnly if there is nothing but vulturous hunger for fine wines, valet reputation, and gilt carriages discoverable there. Of hearts made by the Almighty God I will not believe such a thing. Deep-hidden under wretchedest God-forgetting cants, epicurisms, dead sea-apisms; forgotten as under foulest fat Lethe mud and weeds, there is yet, in all hearts born unto this God's world, a spark of the Godlike still slumbering.

And again, my friend :—

Buccaneers, Choctaw Indians, whose supreme aim in fighting is that they may get the scalps, the money—that they may amass scalps and money—out of such comes no chivalry, and never will. Out of such come only gore and wreck, infernal rage and misery, desperation quenched in annihilation. Behold it, I bid thee; behold there, and consider. What is it that you have a hundred thousand pound bills laid up in your strong room; a hundred scalps hung up in your wigwam? I value not them or thee.

And yet again :—

Love of men cannot be bought by cash payment; without love men cannot endure to be together.

The incentive of gain !

CHAPTER XVI.

THE quotation at the end of the last chapter brings us naturally to the subject of competition.

Of all the many senseless and brutal theories which you practical men support, Mr. Smith, the most fatuous and bestial is the theory of competition.

I use the word theory advisedly. You practical men are fond of scoffing at all humane systems of thought or government as mere "theories." It is one of the vainest of your vanities to believe that you have no theories at all.

Why, John, you practical men have as many theories as any Socialist. But the distinctive marks of all your theories are their falsity, their folly, and their utter impracticability.

For instance, your practical man swears by political economy. But it is by the political economy of the older writers. It is the science of the men who were only blundering over the construction of a rude and untried *theory.* The later and wiser political economy you practical men either do not know or will not accept. You resemble a railway director who should insist upon having his locomotives made to the exact pattern of Stephenson's "Rocket." Your economy isn't up to date, John. You cannot grasp a new idea—you are so practical.

Well, John, one of the laws of your practical school is the law that "Society flourishes by the antagonism of its individuals."

That is the theory of competition. It means that war is better than peace, that a nation where every man tries to get the better of his neighbour will be happier and wealthier, more prosperous and more enlightened than a nation where every man tries to help his neighbour.

Well, John, you practical men are not usually blessed with nimble wits. Allow me to offer you new readings of a few old proverbs for use in competitive society.

Union is weakness. There's a nice terse motto for you. It means just what is meant by the imbecile axiom that "Society flourishes by the antagonism of its individuals."

A house divided against itself shall stand. How does that suit your practical mind? It is the same idea—the idea upon which all opposition to Socialism is built up.

It is better to make one enemy than a hundred friends.

The greatest good of the smallest number.

Waste not have not.

Seest thou a man diligent in his business, he shall give his wealth to princes.

Only a practical, hard-headed people could listen to such propositions without laughing.

You are not good at theories, my practical friend. This competitive theory is rank blockheadism. Allow me to show you. I will test it first by theory, and then we will see how it comes out in practice.

Suppose two men had to get a cart up a hill. Would they get it up sooner if one tried to push it up whilst the other tried to push it down; or if both men tried to pull it up?

Suppose two men had to catch a colt. Which would be the wiser plan, for each man to try to prevent the other from catching it, or for each man to help the other to catch it?

Suppose a captain had to bring a ship from New York to Liverpool. Would he allow half-a-dozen men to fight for the post of helmsman, or the whole crew to scramble for the job of setting sail?

No, John, he would set his crew in order, and send each man to his proper post.

When there is a fire-panic in a theatre, how do people lose their lives? Is it not by all scrambling and fighting to get through the narrow doors? And the result of such a scramble. Is it not the blocking of the exit? But you must know very well that if the people kept cool, and went out quickly, and in an orderly way, they would all escape.

John, if a hundred men had a hundred loaves of bread, and if they piled them in a heap and fought for them, so that some got more than they could eat, and some got none, and some were trampled to death in the brutal scuffle, *that* would be competition. Were it not for competition the hundred men would be all fed.

That John, is the theory of competition. What do you think of it?

And now let us be practical. You have fallen into the stupid error of supposing that competition is better than co-operation, partly because you have never seen anything but competition in practice, and partly because you have not very clear sight, nor very clear brains.

You know that when a railway company, or a salt company, or a coal company, has a monopoly the public gets worse served than when there are several companies in competition with each other.

And you suppose that because competition beats monopoly therefore competition is better than co-operation.

But if you were not such a dim-eyed and thick-witted person, John, you might have noticed that co-operation and monopoly are not the same things. Co-operation is the mutual helpfulness of all; monopoly is the plundering of the many by the few.

Give one man a monopoly of the coal mines and coals would go up in price; but miners' wages would not.

But there is a great difference, friend Smith, between making the collieries the property of one man, and making them the property of the whole people.

Now the Socialists propose to make them the property of the whole people. And they say that if that were done the price of coals would be the natural price. That is to say, it would be the price of the proper keep of the colliers.

Or, for you'll possibly understand this better, being a practical man, they say that the State could work the coal mines better and more cheaply—with less waste of labour—than could a private firm, or a number of firms in competition.

This is because a great deal of the time and energy of the private firms under competition is spent, not in the production and distribution of coals, but in the effort to undersell and overreach each other.

And fortunately, John, we have one actual example of this existing in the postal and telegraphic departments of the State. For

it is a fact which no one attempts to deny, John, that the post-office manages this branch of the national business a great deal better than it ever was or ever could be managed by a number of small firms in competition with each other.

In an earlier chapter I gave you some idea of the *waste* entailed by competition.

" Elihu," in his excellent penny pamphlet, " Milk and Postage Stamps," deals very fully with this matter. He says :—

Taking soap as an example, it requires a purchaser of this commodity to expend a shilling in obtaining sixpennyworth of it, the additional sixpence being requisite to cover the cost of advertising, travelling, &c.; it requires him to expend 1s. 1½d. to obtain twopennyworth of pills for the same reason. For a sewing machine he must, if spending £7 on it, part with £4 of this amount on account of unnecessary cost; and so on in the case of all widely-advertised articles. In the price of less advertised commodities there is in like manner included as unnecessary cost a long string of middlemen's profits and expenses. It may be necessary to treat of these later, but for the present suffice it to say that in the price of goods as sold by retail the margin of unnecessary cost ranges from 3d. to 10d. in the shilling, and taking an average of one thing with another it may be safely stated that one-half of the price paid is rendered necessary simply through the foolish and inconvenient manner in which the business is carried on.

And then he goes on to show that whereas the soap manufacturers are all for competition in the sale of the soap, they will have no competition in the making of soap. As thus :—

Outside his works competition appears quite natural, but inside he will have no divided effort. If you were to suggest that he would supply himself better and more cheaply with boxes by having three joiners' shops working independently of each other and under separate managements, he would tell you that you were an ass, John, and would not be far wrong.

Mr. C. Hart, in a twopenny pamphlet, one of the best I have seen, called " Constitutional Socialism," goes into the same question. He says :—

(a) A and B are two builders, living ten miles apart. A gets a job close to B's house, and B a job close to A's house. All the transport of their ladders and planks is useless work, which, together with that of other builders, necessitates the construction of many useless carts. This reasoning applies to most merchants, canvassers, and shopkeepers (not all of them) who cross each other in every town, and from one town and country to another, uselessly. How many useless ships we have to build on this account!

(b) A country requires industrial and agricultural produce, inland and foreign. Instead of consulting the statistics of consumption, and of writing a few letters to ask for the required number of tons, which would be sent to a central depôt for distribution to the shops, we have thousands of merchants and brokers who each order many separate parcels large and small, a small parcel requiring as much correspondence, bookkeeping, and drafts as a large one. Now, as we could, under Socialism, order a hundred big parcels at once, and thus issue one big draft instead of a thousand small ones, and do a hundred times less correspondence and bookkeeping than these merchants, it follows that nearly all their work is useless, as well as that of their countless dependents, direct and indirect, viz., those who do the useless correspondence and bookkeeping, who build the useless offices, who manufacture the useless office furniture and stationery, who construct and drive the useless carts for this furniture and for all these small parcels, who build the useless banks for those small drafts, who do more useless bookkeeping there, who carry the useless business letters through the post, who act as useless porters, &c., &c. Socialism does not wish to abolish all these middlemen, but only the useless ones.

Frank Fairman, in his "Socialism made Plain," says:—

The immense extension of the telegraph system since it has been managed by the State, and no longer dependant upon the expectation of immediate profit to capitalists, is only an instance of what might be done with regard to telephones, the electric light, railway communication, and many other things; for some of which the public, under the existing system, are called upon to pay, in the shape of interest on capital absolutely wasted in jobbery, promotion money, Parliamentary conflicts, and what is called insurance against risk of loss. as much as it would have cost to do the entire work themselves.

Nor are this increase of cost and waste of labour the only evils of the competitive system. There is also the enormous amount of *profit* made by the private firms to be considered.

This profit comes out of the pockets of the workers and goes into the pockets of the idlers. And by the idlers it is wasted, as I will show you in a future chapter.

But there is another very serious evil due to competition. Please to read the following extract from Mr. H. M. Hyndman's penny pamphlet, "Socialism and Slavery":—

To take a single but very important instance of the way in which our present system works ruin all round. Industrial crises occur more and more frequently in each successive generation. The increasing powers of machinery, the greater facility of transport and communication, do but serve to make matters worse for the mass of the workers in all countries, insomuch that the uncertainty of employment is greatly increased by these recurring crises, apart from the danger of the workers being driven out on to the streets by the introduction of new labour-saving machines. But these crises arise from the very nature of our capitalist system of production. Thus, when a period of depression comes to an end, orders flow in from home and foreign customers; each manufacturer is anxious to take advantage of the rising tide of prosperity, and produces as much as he can, without any consultation with his fellows or any regard for the future: there is a great demand for labourers in the factories, workshops, shipyards, and mines; prices rise all along the line, speculation is rampant; new machines are introduced to economise labour and increase production. All the work is being done by the most thorough social organisation and for manifestly social purposes; the workers are, as it were, dovetailed into one another by that social and mechanical division of labour, as well as by the increasing scale of factory industry. But they have no control whatever over their products when finished. The exchange is carried on solely for the profit of the employing class, who themselves are compelled to compete against one another at high pressure in order to keep their places. Thus a glut follows and then a depression of trade, when millions of men are out of work all over the world, though ready to give their useful labour in return for food; and the capitalists are unable to employ them because the glut which they themselves have created prevents production at a profit.

Competition, it thus appears, raises the price of commodities, lowers the rate of wages, and throws vast numbers of men out of work.

Another evil of the competitive system is the milking of new ideas by the capitalist. Under competition a new invention is a "trade secret," and is worked for the benefit of one firm.

Brown gets hold of a new method of cutting screws which enables him to dispense with half the labour. He conceals this from Jones and Robinson and uses it to undersell them. Let us trace the action of such an invention under competition and under Socialism.

Suppose that labour equals 50 per cent. of the cost of making the screws, and that the new process saves half the labour. That gives Brown a profit of 25 per cent. more than Jones and Robinson. Now, Brown first of all discharges half his men, and then lowers the price of his screws 10 per cent. The results of these operations are:—

1. The public get their screws 10 per cent. cheaper.
2. Brown makes 15 per cent. more profit.

3. Jones and Robinson lose their trade.
4. Half of Brown's men are out of employment.
5. If Brown can *ruin* Jones and Robinson and take all their trade, then he will throw half of their men out of employment and may even raise the price of screws again, and so take all the advantage of the invention.

And very likely Brown has bought this invention from some poor man for a couple of ten pound notes.

Nor does the evil end here. I have it on good authority that in some trades the capitalists have a fund for the purpose of ruining inventors. This is done by a system of law-suits and appeals which make it impossible for a man to work his invention unless he has a great deal of money. This kind of villainy is protected by the libel laws. I will therefore leave you to find out the facts for yourself.

But now consider the result of our new screw-cutting process under Socialism.

A workman invents a new process. He is rewarded by a medal and the naming of the process after its inventor, and the invention becomes the property of the State.

What are the effects? Screws can be made 25 per cent. more cheaply. Who gets the advantage of that?

The people get the advantage of it. You may

1. Reduce the hours of labour in the screw trade by one half, or
2. Send half the screw-cutters to some other work, as farming.

But in either case the people will reap the benefit. For either hours of work will be shorter, or more wealth will be poured into the common store as a consequence of every new invention.

Doubtless, John, some of your political, hard-headed, practical friends will affect to be shocked at the idea that the inventor of our new process gets "no more substantial reward" than a medal and a name. But remember one or two things.

1. The inventor has, already, as much of all substantial things as he requires.
2. That he could not spend money if he got it.
3. That he is under no obligation to think of the future, as he and his wife and children are sure of the care of the State.

Besides, you may remind your practical friends, Mr. Smith, that the heroes of the life-boats, the hospitals, the coalmines, and the battlefield, seldom get so much as a medal or a name.

The heroes who defended Rorke's Drift were rewarded by a grant to each man of a pair of eight-shilling trousers; the heroes of the glorious charge at Balaclava have many of them died in the workhouse.

One other instance of the bad effects of competition, and I have done with the subject.

On the 17th of June, 1893, the *Clarion* quoted from *The New Nation* the following paragraph:

"As soon as I get up a good thing, say in chocolate," says a merchant, "some rival will imitate it in quality and sell it at a lower rate. To hold my own I've to cut his price, but as I can't do that and make a profit, I must adulterate the article a little. He knows the dodge and he will do the same thing. So we go, cutting at each other, until both of our articles are so cheap and poor that nobody will buy them. Then I start the pure goods again, under another name, and the whole circus has to be gone over again."

Every man who knows anything of trade knows how general is the knavish practice of adulteration. As a Lancashire man, you, Mr. Smith, will need no lecture on the evils of calico-sizing. Now, all adulteration is directly due to competition.

Do you doubt it? Allow me to prove my statement by quoting from a speech by John Bright. John Bright was a great apostle of gradgrindery. He was a champion of competition, an opponent of the factory acts and trade unionism; and in the speech to which I allude he intended to excuse adulteration, and he said:—

Adulteration is only another form of competition.

There, Mr. Smith, could anything be clearer? Could any irony, or any argument, or any invective of a Socialist wound competition so deeply as does this maladroit chance-blow of its champion, John Bright?

I notice, Mr. Smith, that there is a statue of John Bright in the Town Hall Square of Manchester. That statue is well placed. John Bright was the natural hero of the cotton age. In our Merrie England we shall most likely prefer to put up memorials to men like John Ruskin and Thomas Carlyle.

CHAPTER XVII.

ONE of the favourite arguments of the Gradgrinds in support of competition is the theory of the Survival of the Fittest. They say that those who fail, fail because they are not fitted to succeed. They say that those who succeed, succeed because they are "fit." They say it is the law of nature that the weakest shall go to the wall, and to the wall with them—and no quarter.

The slumites live in the slums because they are unfit to live anywhere else. The Duke of Marlborough lived in a palace because the intellectual and moral superiority of such a man naturally forced him into a palace.

Burns was a ploughman; Bunyan was a tinker; Lord Chesterfield was a peer. The composer of the popular waltz, "The Masher's Dream," makes ten thousand a year, and lives in a mansion. Richard Jefferies and James Thomson died poor and neglected.

Jay Gould had boundless wealth and tremendous power. Walt Whitman had a modest competence, and no power at all. Or, as the most vivid example I can give you of the great law of the survival of the fittest, let me remind you that Brigham Young was a prophet and a ruler, wealthy and honoured; and that Christ lived a mendicant preacher, and died the death of a felon.

And all these things are justified by the glorious law that the fittest shall survive.

But let me give you my own explanation of the law as to the survival of the fittest. Of two plants or animals, that one will survive which is fittest to endure the conditions in which both exist. The question of which man shall survive depends upon the conditions under which the men shall struggle for survival.

According to the law of nature the man who is best suited by the conditions of the country and the society he lives in will be best fitted to succeed.

In a nation of marauders, then, who live by spoliation and the sword, the fittest to survive would be a different type of man from him who gets first place in a nation of traders, where fierceness and strength of arm are less called for than tenacity and clearness of head.

It thus appears that when we say our poor are poor because they are not fitted to gain wealth, we mean that they are not "fit" to gain wealth under the conditions of life now existing. But under different conditions of life they might succeed.

If, then, the present conditions of life in England are right, the poor are wrong; but if the present conditions of life are not right, the poor are *wronged*.

Therefore, it seems that this theory of the Survival of the Fittest is no answer to our indictment against Society. It proves nothing except that if the poor are unworthy they are unworthy. The question are they unworthy, or is it the arrangement of Society that is unworthy, has still to be answered.

One condition of society enables one kind of man to succeed; another condition of society enables another kind of man to succeed. Now would you say that was the best condition of society that gave to the lowest type of humanity the pre-eminence? Or would you say that was the best condition of society that gave the highest type of humanity the pre-eminence?

Granting that the noblest is really the most proper to survive, is it not desirable that the conditions of society should be so moulded and arranged that noble qualities shall have full play and base qualities be kept in check?

I think that is clear enough, and I now ask you to consider whether society, as it is at present constituted, enables the law of the Survival of the Fittest to work for evil or for good.

For hundreds of ages we have been imprisoning, murdering, prosecuting, and starving our Brunos, our Pauls, our Socrates, our Raleighs, our Joans of Arc, and have heaped rewards and honours on our Alexanders, our Bonapartes, our Jay Goulds, our Rothschilds. Are we to go on for ever in the worship of usury and slaughter and intrigue? Are we still to make the basest the fittest to survive?

To bless power above benevolence? Shall we
never have done admiring and obeying our
Brigham Youngs, nor crucifying our Christs,
nor scorning those who follow Him, and such
as He?

No sensible man would attempt to oppose a
law of nature. *All* natural laws are right.
No natural law can be resisted. But before
we give to any law implicit obedience we shall
be wise to examine its credentials. Natural
laws we *must* obey. But don't let us mistake
the hasty deductions of erring men for the
unchanging and triumphant laws of Nature.
Let us begin, in this case, by asking whether
the law of prey, which seems to be a natural
and inevitable statute among the brutes, has
any right of jurisdiction in the courts of
humanity. Is there any difference between
man and the brutes? If there is a difference,
in what does it consist?

We need not get into a subtle investigation
on this matter. It is sufficient to use common
terms, and say that man has intellect; animals
only instinct. Consider the consequences of
this difference. We have spoken and written
language, which beasts have not. We have
imagination, which beasts have not. We have
memory, history, sciences, religions, which
beasts have not. And we have intellectual
progress, which beasts have not. I might go a
great deal deeper into this matter; but I want
to keep to plain speech and simple issues.
Man has *reason;* beasts have not.

Now reason is a natural thing in man.
Nature gave him reason, because reason is
necessary to the working-out of his development, and I mean to say that by reason we
are to be guided, and not by the law of prey,
which is a natural check and balance put upon
unreasoning creatures. By how much a man's
reason excels a brute's instincts is the man
better than the brute. By how much one man's
reason excels that of his fellows is he better
than they. By how much any policy of
human affairs is more reasonable than another
policy is it best fitted to survive.

It seems, then, that the law of the Survival
of the Fittest does apply to mankind; but it
works with them in a manner different to that
in which it works with the brutes. Well, I
say that our Gradgrinds apply a natural law in

an unnatural manner. That they would rule
mankind by brutal methods.

Before we go any further with this theory
of the Survival of the Fittest, let me ask you
one question. Will you tell me, Mr. Smith,
who *are* the fittest to survive? A great deal
depends upon our answer to that question.

All wealth is got by plunder. If instead of
making laws to stop the depredations of the
sweater we repealed the laws for the repression
of the garrotter, we should soon fall into
anarchy—that is, into a state of savagery, such
as is understood by the word anarchy. The
race to the swift. The battle to the strong.
The weak to the wall. The vanquished to the
sword. A perfect realisation of the Survival
of the Fittest. Then the man with the most
strength and ferocity would take by force of
arms the goods of the weak and timid—and
their lives. Which all of us would call sheer
plunder. But commercialism is just a war of
wits—a gambling or fighting with weapons of
parchment and the like, and really plunder by
force of cunning instead of by force of arms.
And *both* these forms of plunder are forms in
which the baser intellect and the more brutal
physique will always be successful. In personal
conflict, Socrates would be no match for J.
L. Sullivan; in commerce, Jesus Christ would
be exploited by Jay Gould—as he *was*, in fact,
by Judas.

For the Gradgrinds to invoke the laws of
Nature is odd. Our "Survival-of-the-Fittest"-
men declare their dependence on the laws of
Nature, and when anyone suggests a change in
English laws and customs for the sake of the
poor and heavy laden, these barbarian ranters
answer, "Oh, no. You must not meddle with
the laws of Nature. Nature's processes are
inevitable, and cannot be altered by acts of
Parliament." But we *have* laws, and these
wiseacres would keep those laws. If we suggested that no laws should be, they would call
us anarchists. But what shall we call them
who cry out that natural law is the only law,
and yet insist upon the necessity for human
laws as well?

Is there any natural obstacle to the establishment of a community on just terms? Is
there any known law of nature that denies
bread to the industrious and forces wealth

upon the idle? If a natural law makes waste and want imperative, what is that law? Tell me, that I may know it? Natural law as far I *do* know it is against this unjust distribution. Natural law punishes gluttony, and as ruthlessly punishes privation. Nature racks the gourmand and the sluggard with gout, or disfigures him with dropsy, and the starveling and the unresting drudge she visits with consumption and with pestilence. She strikes the miser with a Midas curse—turning his bowels to gold, and she brands the drunkard, the libertine, and the brawler with the mark of the beast. Nature everywhere ordains *temperance*. How, then, can wealth or indulgences be justified in her name? How can we say that the millions of poor slain by unnatural conditions of life are the victims of nature's laws?

To whose interest is it that the poor should suffer? Do their sorrow and travail confer an atom of benefit on any of God's creatures? Injustice is a thing accursed. It does not, never did, and never will confer a benefit on any man. The man who does an injustice suffers for it in his moral nature. He gains nothing, though he makes wealth. For no man can use more than he needs, and Justice would give all men that. The men to whom an injustice is done suffer, and be they many or few, Society suffers because of their suffering.

The Survival of the Fittest is a question of conditions. It can have no great power in the England of to-day. The Survival of the Fittest is another name for Anarchy. Our Society is one bound by law. The unfettered "right of individual enterprise" is anarchy. And it is bad. It is bad because in a state of social warfare, warfare to extermination point, the basest and the vilest have the advantage, for the vile man and the base will fight with less ruth and fewer scruples.

So much for the survival of the fittest. So much for *Laissez Faire*. The man who accepts the *Laissez Faire* doctrine would allow his garden to run wild, so that the roses might fight it out with the weeds and the fittest might survive.

CHAPTER XVIII.

ANOTHER stock argument against Socialism is the assertion that it would destroy all intellectual progress. Here is a quotation from an article by the late Charles Bradlaugh:—

I object to Socialism because it would destroy the incentives which have produced, amongst other things, the "clever" men who serve society in various fashions, as doctors, engineers, architects, and teachers. I am inclined to doubt whether, if the enormous army of Socialist officials were rewarded at the like rate with the scavenger and the ploughman, the temptation on them might not be very great to help themselves to extra recompense from the national stores.

The first sentence in this passage displays a singular misconception of human nature; the second a grotesque misconception of Socialism.

We will dispose of the second sentence first. You will observe that Mr. Bradlaugh spoke of "the enormous army of Socialist officials." He seems to have supposed, as so many suppose, that under Socialism we should be over-run with officials. You will find the same comical blunder in Richter's book.

Now the fact is that under Socialism there would be as few officials, and as many workers, as possible. I don't think you will find the officials in the Post Office more numerous than in any ordinary business house.

But the surprising part of it is that a really shrewd man like Mr. Bradlaugh should have failed to notice the enormous number of officials, and useless officials, too, who burden every department of trade under competition.

For what are all the clerks, travellers, agents, canvassers, salesmen, managers, capitalists, and other costly and needless people but an "enormous army" of officials? Just glance back at the chapter on Competition, and then consider whether Socialism, however badly managed, could possibly add to the number of overpaid and unnecessary non-producers.

Then Mr. Bradlaugh was terribly shocked by the idea that a doctor should be paid at the same rate as a scavenger. This is chiefly due to two misconceptions of Mr. Bradlaugh's. First of all, he had been so used to the recognised money standard of honour that he didn't seem able to realise that a man might, under Socialism, be honoured more for what he *was*, or for what he *did*, than for what he *got*. Secondly, he was so used to seeing such men as scavengers overworked, underpaid, and generally despised, that it did not occur to him as possible that under Socialism every worker would be treated justly, and respected as a man. But turn the idea the other way round, and you can reply to Mr. Bradlaugh's objection that it will be a decidedly good society for the average man where the scavenger or ploughman is as well paid as the doctor or the engineer. However, I shall have more to say about our friend the scavenger in a future chapter.

Another amusing blunder of Mr. Bradlaugh's is the idea that if an official got no more pay than a scavenger he would turn thief and rob the public stores.

That seems to imply that the "clever" men, the men whom Mr. Bradlaugh evidently regarded as the salt of the earth, are not, in his opinion, very honest. If an underpaid clerk, in these times, robs his employer he is sent to prison—as a rogue. We hear nothing about the injustice of society or the folly of competition in paying him no more than a scavenger.

But, observe, once more, that it could only be under Ideal Socialism that the official and the scavenger would be equally paid. Therefore, there would be nothing for the official to steal but food or clothing, and as every man would have as much of those as he needed for the asking, I don't see what an official would gain by stealing more.

No. The error arises, once more, from a misconception of Socialism. The fact is, our critics will keep supposing that under Socialism the workers would be as badly treated and as badly rewarded as they are now.

Let us turn, then, to Mr. Bradlaugh's first sentence. Socialism, he says, "would destroy the incentives which have produced the clever men who serve society." This is the old story about the incentive of gain. It comes very

curiously from the mouth of Mr. Bradlaugh. Very curiously indeed.

Mr. Bradlaugh was a very clever man, and he had worked very hard. Was gain *his* incentive? No one who knows anything of his life will suppose so for a moment. It is a marvellous thing. Here we had a man who had fought a bitter, a terrible, and uphill battle all his life long for *principle*, a man who was faithful unto death, and who died poor and embarrassed, and we find him objecting to Socialism because it would remove the incentive of *gain*.

But there is the statement, and it is a common one. Mr. Morley repeats it. Mr. Morley is convinced that if existence were no longer a sordid struggle for money the genius of the people would die out, and we should sink into barbarism and retain nothing but the bare necessaries of life.

Well, this is what I call comic. Mr. Morley seems satisfied with things as they are. What do his words assume? They assume :—

1. That the greatest and noblest of the race are actuated by avarice. Which is not true.
2. That the greatest and noblest of the race secure the most *wealth*. Which is not true.
3. That the people are at present in the enjoyment of more than the necessaries of life. Which is not true.
4. That the people are at present in the enjoyment of civilisation and refinement. Which is not true.
5. That Socialism would discourage genius and patriotism. Which is not true.
6. That Socialism would encourage idleness. Which is not true.

I will take these six errors in their order and refute them.

The first is the assertion that if a clever man were not paid higher *wages* than a manual labourer he would refuse to devote his talents to the service of society.

Now, John, out of their own mouths shall these men be condemned.

Have you ever read any of the speeches and articles on the Payment of Members of Parliament? You have. What is the stock argument used against the payment of members?

It is the argument that to pay members would be to lower the tone and impair the quality of the House of Commons. It is the argument that *men of talent will serve the nation better for honour than for money!*

I think, John, I have them on the hip. This argument is used by the same men who tell us that Socialism would degrade the nation by abolishing the incentive of gain.

With how little wisdom is the world governed. What do you think of the morality, what do you think of the intelligence, what do you think of the knowledge of these " practical statesmen," John Smith; these men you cheer and vote for?

They tell you one day that unless you pay clever men big wages they will cease to work.

They tell you another day that if you pay clever men at all they will cease to work.

They declare first of all that it is only the base lust after dirty *money* that makes men great.

They declare next that money is such a vile thing that if you pay members of Parliament you will ruin the country, because only greedy adventurers will work for money.

Is the swinish lust for wealth the one motive power of all clever men, John, *except* our members of Parliament?

What think you is the chief food of genius? Does the prospect of wealth inspire Hamlets or Laocoons, and steam-engines, and printing presses? The true artist, the man to whom all creative work is due, is mainly inspired, sustained, and rewarded by a love of his art. Milton wrote " Paradise Lost " for £8. Can greed produce a poem like it? Many improvements in machinery are made by workmen. Often they get no profit. Sometimes the master patents the improvement, pays the drudge a few shillings a week for his ideas, and makes thousands. Shall we measure men's brains like corn, or gauge the pressure and the power of fiery passions and quenchless faiths by the horse-power. All the forces of all the kings of the earth cannot make one brave man turn on his heel; all the wealth of the nations cannot buy one pure soul; all the fools in a big city cannot conquer one strong brain; all the drilled and crammed dunces that political economy and hide-bound school systems can band together cannot advance the cause of knowledge or liberty one inch.

Was it greed made Socrates expound philosophy, or Shakspeare write plays? Was it competition made Watt invent the steam-engine, or Davy the safety-lamp, or Wheatstone the telegraph? Was it greed that abolished slavery? Was it greed made Darwin devote his life to science? Was it greed that unfolded the secrets of astronomy, of geology, and of other important facts of nature? Or did greed give us musical notation, the printing press, the pictures of Turner and Raphael, the poems of Spenser, and the liberties and privileges of the English Constitution?

The true artist: He to whom all creative work is due is mainly inspired, sustained, and rewarded by a love of his art. He will take money, for he must live. He will take money, for money is the badge of victory. But with or without money, and with or without praise, he will worship the beloved mistress, art. He calls his wealthy patrons Philistines, and in his soul despises them.

This paltry plea about *pay!* Yet, even if we admit that "pay" is the one prize and the one incentive of life, it would seem as though the men of "ability" are not the men who get the most of it. It may seem a sad thing that a Darwin should get no more "pay" than the "clod" who breaks stones. But there are "clods" who break backs and hearts, instead of stones, who get paid more than the men of ability in question. For instance, Jay Gould, the "financier," got more "pay" and held more wealth than Gladstone, and Carlyle, and Darwin, and Koch, and Galileo, and Columbus, and Cromwell, and Caxton, and Stephenson, and Washington, and Raphael, and Mozart, and Shakespeare, and Socrates, and Jesus Christ ever got between them. *So* perfect is the present system of "pay."

Are the best men of to-day the best paid? Are the most useful men the best paid? Are the most industrious men the wealthiest? Do the noblest and the cleverest men work for gain? Do they get rich? Do the great mass of the labouring classes work for gain? Do *they* get rich? Did the love of gain ever make a hero or a martyr? Did it ever win a battle? Will a man do most for love or for money, for honour or for money, for duty or for money? Having no money, does a genius become a fool? Having much money, does a fool become a genius? Did any nation, loving money, ever become great; or, gaining riches and luxury, ever remain great? It has been written that:—

> Romans in Rome's quarrel
> Spared neither land nor gold,
> Nor child, nor wife, nor limb, nor life,
> In the good days of old.

But it has never been written nor said nor known of any but the vilest and meanest savages that they would sell their country or their wives or their children or their faiths for *money.*

Is there any community as united and as effective as a family? The family is the soundest, the strongest, and the happiest kind of society, and next to that is the tribe of families. And why? Because all the relations of family life are carried on in direct opposition to the principles of political economy and the survival of the fittest. A family is bound by ties of love and mutual helpfulness. The weakly child is not destroyed; it is cherished with extremest tenderness and care. The rule is vested in the parents, and not knocked down to the highest bidder. The brothers do not undersell each other. The women are better treated than the men, not worse, as in the factories, and each member of the family receives an equal share of the common wealth.

But let us return to the article of Mr. Bradlaugh. Here is another statement:—

To me, I avow, it does seem that Sir James Paget or the editor of a newspaper is more valuable than the street-sweeper, that the effort necessary to become a clever doctor or successful journalist is greater than that necessary for an average stone-breaker. Sir Charles Russell, Mr. Burne-Jones, or Mr. Wm. Black may, it appears to me, have each been required to devote years of preliminary study and ardent application which are not required from the omnibus conductor or letter carrier.

Here is the same idea, that services and labour can be recompensed by "pay." The same idea that because one man can do more or better than another he should have more *money;* the same unaccountable inability to see that all the money the earth contains can never buy a man more than the necessaries of life, for a man has but one body to clothe, but one stomach to feed, but one head to rest upon a pillow.

Now, John, if every man had *enough,* would it not be a pitiful spectacle to see the salt of the earth—the men of knowledge and ability—whining for more?

Why should a clever man want more than an average worker? If the workman's pay is enough for his wants—and *that* "ought" to be—why should an artist have more? The workman having enough, should the artist have more than enough? He does not *need* it. He cannot use it. He is already more blessed than the workman, for his talent is a boundless source of pleasure to him and his work is a gratification and not a task. A really great-souled man would spurn such a guerdon for his victory. In a healthy state of human feeling, to offer a hero money and vain titles would affront him as surely as offering a man a sugar-stick to eat or a baby's rattle to play with. Virtue is its own reward. The artist's reward is his success; his honour is his works. The true hero asks for service, not for pay. "Ich Dien" is the real Prince's motto all the world over. I'll have to look up a list of biographies, so that Smith and Co. may know what a hero is. They are rather scarce now. And it is curious that at a time when the demand for a hero is very pressing the supply has failed. That now, when heroes could have more gold and more promotion than were ever showered on them before, they do seem strangely loth to show themselves. I cannot explain this, John, unless by supposing that heroes are not ruled by the law of supply and demand, and do not much covet riches or places in the House of Peers.

But let us take some homely illustrations of my contention that merit does not depend upon pay.

You know something about cricket. Take the Notts team. You will find that all the professionals are paid at the same rate. But you will not find them all equally good. Shrewsbury is the best bat in the team. He gets no more *pay* than a less expert man. But does that fact prevent any one of us from recognising his superior power? Do you not see that it is the same in all professions? I daresay Mr. Sims makes more money than

Shakespeare would make now. But we never make a mistake as to which of the two stands at the head of his art. John L. Sullivan, the boxer, got, I am told, £500 a week for acting. But even if that be more than Mr. Irving would get, it does not follow that any man can believe Sullivan to be the better actor.

Homely illustration No. 2: That a man *will* do his best even when he gets no more pay than another of his trade less clever than him-self. Here again we take Shrewsbury as an example. Put him into the Players' eleven. He well get no more money than any other batsman. Yet he is the *best* batsman. But will he therefore not try to score? *Ask* him. *See* him. Yes ; I know what you will say. If he does not do his best he will be thrown out, and then he will get no money. But Mr. Stoddart tries as hard as Shrewsbury, and he gets *no* money. And you will find in the Gentle-men and Players' matches that the Gentlemen are as keen and as anxious to win as are the Players. And you will *always* find that the man who works or fights for love, or honour, or duty, or fame, will work harder and fight more fiercely and bravely than the man who fights for pay. Because the former has his *heart* in the work and the latter has not.

And notice another very curious thing about Mr. Bradlaugh's paragraph.

He tells us that Sir Charles Russell and Mr. William Black have been required to devote years of preliminary study to their trades. He suggests therefore that now they shall be paid extra wages. Why?

Is not all wealth created by labour? How did Messrs. Black and Russell live during their period of education? Who kept them?

They were kept by the workers, and are therefore in debt to the workers, and not the workers to them. But of this more anon.

We may now go back to Mr. Morley. Of his six errors I have answered three. We will take Nos. 3 and 4 together. They imply that the people are at present in the enjoyment of the necessaries of life.

What about the unemployed? What about pauperism? What about sweating? What about the payment of unskilled labour? What about female labour? What about the railway workers, the canal workers, the chemical workers, the costermongers, the dockers, the chain and nail makers, the agricultural labourers? What about the slums? Does Mr. Morley ever read any Blue Books? Does he know *anything* about the condition of this country? If he does he makes very bad use of the knowledge.

Talk about a barbarous society in which men should have but the necessaries of life. Just cast your eye over this brief extract from Dr. Russell's pamphlet on life in one room :—

Of the inhabitants of Glasgow 25 per cent. live in houses of one apartment. . . . No less than 14 per cent. of the one-roomed houses, and 27 per cent. of the two-roomed houses, contain lodgers—strange men and women, mixed up with husbands, and wives, and children, within the four walls of small rooms. . . . There are thousands of these houses which contain five, six, and seven inmates, and hundreds which are inhabited by from eight up to even thirteen. . . . Of all the children who die in Glasgow before they complete their fifth year, 32 per cent. die in houses of one apartment, and not 2 per cent. in houses of five apartments and upwards. . . . From beginning to rapid ending the lives of these children are short parts in a wretched tragedy. . . . I can only venture to lift a corner of the curtain which veils the life which is lived in these houses. It is impossible to show you more.

That is official testimony, and Mr. Morley talks about "necessaries" of life. Do you count fresh air, health, decency, and cleanliness as necessaries? If you do, what say you to the barbarism of Glasgow, of Liverpool, of London, and of Manchester? Come, will you tell me how Socialism is going to ruin Ancoats, or lower the moral standard of Whitechapel, or debase the ideal of Black Country life? It will be time enough for our statesmen to despise the "necessaries of life" when they have made it possible for the people to get them.

Error No. 6, that Socialism would encourage laziness, I shall deal with in a future chapter.

CHAPTER XIX.

THE common misconceptions of Socialism are most perverse and foolish. Mr. Herbert Spencer wrote an article called "The Coming Slavery." I think he is responsible for the much-quoted opinion that Socialism would result in a more odious form of slavery than any the world has yet known.

Clearly there are two things which Mr. Herbert Spencer, like most of our critics, has failed to understand. One of these things is Socialism; the other is the condition of existing society.

I deny that Socialism would result in any form of slavery at all; and I assert that a most odious form of slavery exists at present in this so-called free country. Let us see.

First, as to Socialism. Mr. Spencer's idea appears to be that under Socialism the State would compel men to work against their will, or to work at occupations uncongenial to them. This is a mistake. The State would not compel any man to work. It would only enable all men to work, and to live in peace and comfort by their labour.

If a man did not choose to work he would not be coerced. He could either do his fair share of the work of the community in return for his fair share of the wealth, or he could decline to work.

But if he declined to work he would certainly have to starve, or to leave the State.

Now I want to point out to you, before I go any further, that as things are at present some men live luxuriously and do no work, many men do a great deal of work and live wretchedly, and nearly three-quarters of a million of men who are willing to work can get no work to do.

To hear people talk about slavery under Socialism, you would suppose we had freedom now. Robert Ingersoll says :—

Some of the best and purest of our race have advocated what is known as Socialism. . . . Socialism seems to me to be one of the worst possible forms of slavery. . . . Nothing would so utterly paralyse all the forces, all the splendid ambitions and aspirations that tend now to the civilisation of man. . . . Socialism destroys the family and sacrifices the liberties of all. If the Government is to provide work it must decide for the worker what he must do, &c. Is it possible to conceive of a despotism beyond this ? The human race cannot afford to exchange its liberty for any possible comfort.

The human race cannot afford to exchange its liberty for any possible comfort ! But the human race has not got any liberty to exchange. The human race, at least the great majority, are *slaves*.

But ask yourself, Mr. John Smith, what liberty of choice is left to you. Suppose you are out of work, can you have work for the asking ? No. But under Socialism you could always have work. Is *that* a proof of slavery ? Suppose under Socialism you were told that you must work or starve ! Would that be any more despotic treatment than the treatment you get now ? Tell your present employers that you do not wish to work, and see what the alternative will be. You must work or starve now. The difference between present conditions, and the conditions of Socialism are that you now work long hours for a bare existence, whereas in a Socialistic State you would work short hours for a life of honour and comfort.

The Socialistic State would not compel any man to work ; it would prevent him from living on the work of others. It would organise the industries, production and distribution, of the community, and would then say to the citizen, " If you would enjoy the benefits and share the wealth of this commonwealth you must also obey the laws and share the labour." Surely that is just. But in no case can it be twisted to mean slavery, for the man who did not like the conditions could refuse them, just as he can now.

But note that other statement of Mr. Ingersoll's :—

If the Government is to provide work it must decide for the worker what he must do.

Must it ? Why ?

At present the capitalist finds work, but he does not decide what we must do. He cannot decide, or he would.

So when the State found work it would not decide what each man must do.

You will ask me how a Socialist State would apportion the work. I ask *you* how the work is apportioned *now*.

You have a son, say a lad of fourteen, and wish to put him to a trade. You ask him his choice. He says he would like to be a cabinet-maker. You apply at the shops in your own town and you find that trade is bad, or that the allowed number of apprentices is made up. So you get the boy work as an engineer or a painter.

That is to say, your boy can choose his trade *subject to the demand for labour of certain kinds.* If all the boys wanted to be engineers they could not all get work at that trade.

These conditions would exist under Socialism. The state, or the municipality, would need a certain number of plumbers and a certain number of painters. If more boys asked to be painters than the State needed to do its painting some of those boys would have to take other work. Where does the slavery come in?

Robert Ingersoll is considered a very able man, and Herbert Spencer enjoys the reputation of being a great thinker.

What have these famous men been doing with their eyes? How have they contrived to commit the egregious blunder of supposing that men have free choice of occupation now? How many men do you know, John Smith, who are working at the trade of their choice, or living where and how they please?

Let us return to your boy of fourteen. Suppose, instead of choosing to be a cabinet-maker, he said, "I want to be a doctor!" You would laugh at him. Why?

Because it is absurd for a weaver's son to ask to be a doctor. Why?

Because it costs a lot of money to become a doctor. And, once more, why?

Because a doctor has a great deal to learn, and education is *dear*.

So though your son wishes to be a doctor, though he might possess great talent for the work, he must go and be a candlestick-maker instead, for you are too poor to give him his choice.

But under Socialism education would be free. It would be free to *all*. Therefore the competition for doctorships would be equal. It would not be what it is now—a close thing for the privileged classes. So your boy would have as good a chance as any other.

"Ah," but you will say, "under Socialism *all* the boys would want to be doctors and artists and writers." Very likely. And at present all the boys want to be "gentlemen," but very few of them get their wish, and many of them have to be beggars—or thieves.

Under Socialism any boy who had the industry and talent might qualify himself to get a diploma. Of course, when he had got it he might not get an appointment as one of the medical men for his town.

But I understand that there are at present a good many doctors with no practice.

There is no greater blunder possible than the blunder of supposing that in this country at the present time every man may follow the work of his choice. It is a ridiculous error.

To read Mr. Bradlaugh, Mr. Ingersoll, and Mr. Spencer, you would think that things are so well ordered now that all kinds of work must fall to the men best fitted to do it.

I don't want to be rude, but the books and articles I have quoted from certainly suggest that some of the men who are writers and philosophers to-day were meant by nature for a very different kind of work.

Writers and painters, Mr. Smith, have to write and paint what they can *sell*; provided they can get a chance to write and paint at all.

Take my own case. Here I am, after being forty-two years a free man in a free country, obliged to confess that I have never yet succeeded in doing the kind of work I have wanted to do.

Turn your eyes to trade. There are two carpet factories in a town. Another man sets up in that trade. What happens? He may be a good man, and a clever man; and he may make better carpets than the other firms, but unless he is very rich they will ruin him by selling below cost price in order to retain the trade in their own hands.

Or suppose there are two papers in a town and a rival paper is started. What will happen?

The new paper may be a much better paper

than the old ones, but unless its proprietor is a rich man it cannot live. Why?

Because there is such a thing as a boycott. The proprietors of the established papers will send around to the news-agents and say, " If you sell the *Comet* I will take away the agency for the *Fog Horn*," and " If you sell the *Comet* I shall get fresh agents for the *Welsher*."

Now suppose the agent is poor, as most agents are, and suppose he is selling both those papers and clearing ten shillings a week on the sale. Is it likely that he will risk the ten shillings for the sake of selling a good paper which may not pay him one shilling or may not live a month?

Do you call that agent a free agent? Do you mean to say that the would-be proprietor of the *Comet* is a free man, or that he can do what work he pleases?

Under present conditions, John, rascality and money can always overreach honesty and brains.

I am not talking fine-spun theory now, like that of Robert Ingersoll. I am telling you *facts* and arguing from experience.

About a year ago I met the manager of a weekly London paper. He told me that he was trying to establish a circulation in the provinces, but that the local papers had boycotted him. And then he said, "We are making some headway, and have got a small sale; but every copy of our paper we sell costs us *four shillings* to dispose of."

You will observe, John, that the merit of the papers had nothing to do with the case. The London paper was certainly better than its local rivals. But the locals had blocked the agents and lowered their prices.

Talk about slavery! Freedom of contract! Under your much-glorified freedom of contract, how many contracts are freely made? Under your vaunted liberty of the Individual, how many individuals have any liberty at all? At this present day in this fine country the bulk of the people are slaves. They are slaves *not* to a wise, beneficent, and popular Government, but to a ring of greedy, grasping fools; a coterie of rich barbarians—who would boil down the last nightingale if they thought his bones would serve to dye yarn; who would choke up the last well if they had no place handy in

which to shoot their alkali dust, and would cover the last rood of sward with ashes, if they thought there was no hope of grinding the said ashes with sewer slime to make |mortar for the people's houses. "Can any one imagine a despotism more terrible" than the regulation of work by Government? I think so. I think I could find it. But I have no need to look. See; it is here, ready to my hand.

It is here, in a letter, long kept by me, a sample of many I constantly receive:—

If you can see your way to give us poor devils of silk dyers a word or two I am sure it would do us good. We work longer hours than any others in the trade in England, get less wages, and, for our lives,. or rather our situations, dare not openly belong to a union. If we strike—as we did last summer—pressure is brought upon us by our wives and children (nearly all of whom have to work) being dismissed from their situations. If we write to the *Leek Times*—the best friend we poor dyers ever had—we are afraid to sign our names; and if we have a meeting it has to be kept a dead secret. In fact, it is not worth living to work under such circumstances, and as far as I can see the only union we shall ever get will be the union workhouse, and many of us are half way there now. Give us a word to strengthen the fearful and encourage the weak. Somebody must help us. We cannot help ourselves. We have been down so long that we don't know how to get up.

P.S.—For God's sake *do not mention my name.*

For God's sake, *do not mention my name.* What? It is no crime to write to a pressman and say, " I am not happy," or " I am ill-paid." It is not against the law to say, " We have no union." If a man trembles to hear his own name given with his own true statements, what becomes of the sacred "liberty of the individual"? Is *this* your liberty, then? Is this the liberty *we* "cannot sacrifice for any comfort"? Are these the noble aspirations and glorious ambitions that Socialism would trample out of life? Is this free England's free choice? When a free man fears to speak his own name? Surely there is *some* despotism even now extant.

But Mr. Ingersoll says, "The human race cannot afford to sell its liberty for any possible comfort." I have, I think, said enough to satisfy you that the human race have no liberty to sell, but I don't want you to suppose that Socialism is nothing nobler than a desire for comfort. We want better things than comfort. We want freedom and justice, and honour and education. Your individualist and utilitarian are the disciples of comfort. To their comfort and to their luxury all that is best and sweetest in the lives of the poor is sacrificed. *They* imagine that so long as the worker has enough to eat and drink he has all that he requires. The comfort they wot of is the comfort of the hog—an overfed stomach, a bed of straw, and a close and filthy stye. We Socialists ask that the people shall be held as something better than hogs. We ask that they shall be treated as men and women—and to men and women comfort is not the fulfilment of life.

The people need more than wages. They need *leisure*. They need culture. They need humane and rational amusement. They need the chance to exercise those " splendid ambitions and aspirations " about which our critic is eloquent.

I want to know why the collier and the weaver and the railway drudge and the silk dyer should be doomed to a dull and brutish round of labour—I will not call it work—and greasy stew, and bad beer, and straw mattress, and filthy slum ? I want to know why the yahoo yelping of the free and easy should be considered recreation ; and why the promotion to a head shuntership at 21s. should be counted as high enough ambition ? Tell me, why should not the best that art, and science, and literature, and music, and poetry, and the drama can do be placed at the disposal of the humblest workers ? Why should not the factory girl be an educated lady ? Why should the collier not be a cultured gentleman ?

The answer is " Capitalism !" The exigencies of capitalism grind these people down, rob them of rest, of energy, of health, of food, of time—so that they have neither heart nor mind nor opportunity to become aught but drudges. Talk about " splendid ambitions and aspirations ! " Such things now are for the fortunate few ; but we want them for the many.

Beware, Mr. Smith, of mistaking " what is understood as Socialism " for the genuine article. Genuine Socialism would make the collier into a gentleman. " What is understood as Socialism " could only make the gentleman into a collier. There is a difference.

CHAPTER XX.

W HEN Socialists complain of the misery of the poor they are often told by Pressmen, Parsons, and Politicians, that all the sufferings of the poor are due to their own vices and folly. Thus, a short time ago, the Manchester *Examiner and Times*, in reviewing a little book of mine, went out of its way to offer me a lesson in political economy, and announced that the misery of the masses was due " to sin, hereditary and acquired."

The *Examiner* implied, of course, that the misery of the people was due to their own sin.

This is the very reverse of the truth. The misery of the people is due to the sins, negligences, and ignorances of those who rob them of their earnings, and grow rich upon their moral ruin and physical destruction.

Is it true that poverty is the result of idleness, of improvidence, and of vice ?

If it were, then we should always find that the idle, the vicious, and the improvident were poor ; and that the industrious, the thrifty, and the temperate were well off.

But it is a fact that many idle, vicious, and improvident people are rich, and it is a fact that the poorest people in the world are the most industrious, and sober, and thrifty.

Now, John, I want to convince you of two things. Firstly, that the vices of the poor are due to their surroundings, instead of the surroundings being due to the vices ; and, secondly, that universal industry, and thrift, and temperance amongst the poor would tend to make them *poorer* than they now are.

The sins laid to the charge of the poor are three :—

1. Idleness.
2. Improvidence.
3. Drunkenness.

The first charge is a false libel. So far from the poor being criminally idle, they are criminally industrious.

The second charge is a misnomer. The improvidence of the poor is so clearly due to ignorance that it should be called by that name.

The third charge, that of drunkenness, has a greater foundation of truth, although I believe from my personal observation, which has been extensive, that the poor are much more temperate than many of their critics would have us believe.

First of all, let us consider this word industry. You often hear industry praised as a virtue. I think the thing is not a virtue in itself. The virtue lies in the motive and method of its use. There is no virtue in a plough. It is an instrument for good or evil according as it is used for preparing the field for a crop, or for tearing up the garden of an enemy. So with industry. We read of those whose hands are cunning to devise an evil thing, and whose feet are swift to do iniquity. We should not praise a burglar for his industry, though he might rob a dozen villas in a week. If mere *doing* is to get us praise, what laudable and industrious men were Alexander and Buonaparte! They were always working, but the seed they sowed was evil.

Industry is only expedient and valuable for the nation when it produces good fruits. It is only laudable in the individual when inspired by noble motives. You must not suppose that the nations which do the most work are the greatest nations. You must not fall into the error of the economist, and suppose that the people who " produce most" are the greatest or the worthiest people. Before praising a nation for its productiveness and industry, we should inquire if the things they produce are noble or worthless things, and if the labour of their hands is the labour of slaves or of freemen—of artists or of Philistines.

It does not follow that the man who works the hardest is the most industrious man, nor that he deserves much credit for what he does. He may be constrained to work by force of fate. It may be with him a case of work or starve. He may be working for selfish ends only—for greed, or avarice, or ambition, or vanity—as many of us are. Then, if the work of his hands or wits be good work it is expedient, but it is not noble in him. He deserves as little admiration, earns as little reward, and is inspired by motives no higher than those which actuate the money-lender, or the gambler, or the time-serving politician.

The kind of industry worthy of praise is the kind which is useful in its ends and unselfish in its objects. If, in a colony, there were a scarcity of corn ; if a few men owned the land and the rest had to till it for their food ; if the landlords gave only a pound of meal for a day's service, and set the day's service at fourteen hours, the servants would have to work hard. They would have to work like beasts of burden ; or starve, or fight. If they toiled and suffered would you call their slavery industry ? Would you praise and honour them as noble and diligent men ? I should say they are cowards or fools to endure this. I should say their lives are laborious, but not industrious, and that their efforts are no more worthy in them or creditable to them than those of the tram-horse who fags in the shafts all day—for dread of the whipthong in his driver's hand. But *that* is the commonest form of industry in England to-day, and *that* is the kind of industry the peer and pressman, the bishop and the capitalist, have in their minds when they extol the dignity of labour and the virtue of industry, and when they impress upon the minds of the working-class audiences the glory of " honest toil."

Suppose the case changed with our Colony. The land is in the hands of the people, but its yield is meagre and bread is scarce. The working day is fixed at ten hours, that being the time essential to the production of the smallest yield capable of supporting life. Would you call the man who worked his ten hours faithfully day after day—and no more— an industrious man ? Would you say he was a man to praise and admire ? I should say no. This man does his duty and no more ; and it is not a virtue for a man to do his duty, for it would be a sin if he did not do his duty. This man bears the same relation to an industrious man that an honest man bears to a generous one. The honest man pays what is due. That is all his duty—as *he* understands it—demands. If he did less he would be a rogue. But the generous man not only pays what is claimed—he gives what is wanted.

Again, suppose one man to be left to support himself. Though he worked twenty hours a day to get food or luxuries for himself, you would not call that laudable. Because the motive is purely a selfish one, and all the labour is for his own gratification. But this is a form of industry much belauded by our pastors and masters. This lonely, selfish glutton is a man made of the stuff of which very many British *heroes* have been made. He is painfully like the men held up to us as *examples* to copy and as idols to worship. He is the kind of man who "gets on."

Return again to our Colony. The land is the people's. The fixed working hours are ten a day; but the fields are not enough tilled, and the harvests are still poor. Now suppose some man seeing this goes out and works five hours extra daily for the common good, *he* is an industrious man. He is made of the stuff of which real heroes are spun. Or suppose he sees that pick and spade and muscle and bone are overmatched in the struggle to win bread from the obstinate soil, and seeing this gives all his thought and time, sacrifices all his pleasures and desires, to the one task of designing and constructing a plough or other engine to relieve and feed the weary and famished people—well, I say, that is an industrious man; that is a noble man. His work is "honest toil"; he *is* a hero.

Or suppose another case—the case of a man who loves work for its own sake. Here is an artist, say, or a musician. He loves art or music. He labours at his chosen art with all the power he has, with all the thought, and love, and courage, and patience of his nature. With a devotion that no rebuff can shake, with an affection that no triumph can weaken, he stands at his easel or sits at his piano content laboriously and obscurely to create beautiful things for their own sake. Then, I say, that man is an industrious man. He is a man

most valuable to his fellow-creatures, but he is not so exalted a hero as the man described just now.

There is a great difference between work and toil, between task work and work of choice; and this difference—palpable as it is to a man like me, who has tried both forms of labour—is too often lost sight of by moralists who make it their business to preach to the masses.

Between the navvy wheeling interminable barrows of clay over endless miles of planks at a fixed pittance, and the struggling author or painter living on dry bread and dreams in a garret, there is this immense difference, that whereas the navvy's work is a dull, monotonous, uninteresting task, with no motive but that of winning an animal subsistence, no exercise except for the physical powers, and no hope beyond a doubtful promotion to the post of ganger, the work of the painter or the writer, howsoever poor and obscure he be, is a labour of love; a labour that is in itself a pleasure, a recreation, and an education. A work that employs and trains the highest faculties; that inspires the heart and brain with the brightest hopes; that holds out to the poorest and most insignificant of its drudges at least a chance, a little promise, however remote, of the highest honours and the most magnificent rewards.

It is all very well for the business man, the parson, the author, the engineer, the member of Parliament, to abuse the workman as idle, thriftless, and drunken; but let us do the workman justice. Let us remember that his work is neither exciting, pleasing, ennobling, nor remunerative. Often I have heard professional men say, "Talk about the working classes! What do they know of work? They never work as hard as I do. They have not the worry and strain that mental work involves. I am a manufacturer—a doctor—a lawyer—my work is never done." All this is true. The doctor's work or the author's work is never done. But remember that he loves it so much that he would not wish it ever done. He is so wrapped up in it, so wedded to it, that if it were done, if he were obliged to take off the harness and to go to grass in the prime of life, he would actually break his heart.

It is very nice for professional men to boast of their industry and love of work. They are doing the work of their choice. But take them away from the theatre or the desk, the pulpit, or the quarter-deck, and set them to carrying bricks up a ladder, stitching slop clothing, or scribbling out invoices, and see how they will enjoy that, and how industrious they will be.

It is easy to tell a workman to be industrious and contented in that walk of life to which Providence has called him. But it would be neither easy nor pleasant to take his place and show him how it should be done; and I tell you frankly I believe that if Providence called a Prime Minister or a Bishop to dig coals or puddle iron, Providence would have to use a long trumpet or the gentlemen would not hear.

Ask any man of taste and sense which he would prefer—a pitcher with a stencil pattern printed on it, a bad copy multiplied a thousand times of some original design, or the same pitcher moulded in a form peculiar to itself, and ornamented with the original design itself hand-painted, and not repeated on any other piece of pottery extant. He will ell you he prefers the original work.

Now, ask any man of taste and sense whether he would rather tend a machine which should turn out pitchers by the thousand all of one form and colour, or himself turn and mould the clay upon the wheel and under his own hand. Ask any man who knows men and life and understands human nature and human work, whether a number of men or women would rather stamp the same design ten thousand times upon a piece of plaster, or set to work with gouge and chisel and carve out leaves and flowers to their own fancy and design.

In proportion as you can make men's work artistic will it become pleasant and elevating and productive of contentment. In proportion as the work becomes more pleasing, more interesting, and more noble will the people grow to love it ; and the more the people come to love their work, the more industrious and contented will they be. That is one of the practical values of art.

But, again, there is a negative as well as a positive value in art. If a man's work is irksome, brutish, cheerless, and without hope or interest, the man grows jaded and dissatisfied. Getting no hope, no variety, no joy nor excitement out of the labour of his hands and brain, he seeks for change and relaxation elsewhere. He *must* have change and rest and pleasure. The duller and harder his task, the more his thirst for excitement and for ease. Just think of these facts. Remember that by making a man a drudge you make him contract a debt to nature ; and nature will be paid. If you will or must have drudges, you must and shall provide them an antidote to the bane, o: they must and will provide the antidote themselves. You see that, do you not ? Well, there are the drudges drudging all around you. Have you provided them abundance of pure and innocent recreation for their leisure and refreshment ? You have not. But you grant a great many public-house licenses, I notice. You set them an example on the Stock Exchange and in the counting-house and on the racecourse which they *may* follow. And the result —— ?

CHAPTER XXI.

LET us now consider how far drunkenness is responsible for the poverty of the masses. First of all, let me say a few words on drink and drinking. It would be a mistake to suppose that the man who is oftenest drunk is the heaviest drinker. Many a highly-respectable middle-class gentleman spends more money on drink in one day than a labourer earns in a week, yet withal is accounted a steady man. I have seen a journalist, and one very severe upon the vices of the poor, drink eight shillings worth of whiskey and soda in an evening, and do his work correctly. I have known a sailor to sit up all night playing at cards, and consume about a pint of rum and a gallon of stout in the process, and then go out at eight in the morning and score nine consecutive bull's-eyes at 200 yards. But the average poor labourer of the slums would be mad on a quarter of the liquor. Why?

There are three principal reasons :—1. The labourer is often in a low state of health. 2. The labourer does not drink with any caution or method. 3. The labourer does not get pure liquor.

Now I must in justice say for the poor that they have great excuse for drinking, and that they are often blamed for being drunk when they are simply poisoned.

Drunkenness is a disease. It is just as much a disease as typhus fever or cholera, and often arises from very similar causes. Any medical man will tell you that the craving for alcoholic stimulants is frequently found amongst men whose nervous system is low.

But there are, I think, three chief causes of drunkenness. A man may crave for drink when his system is out of order. And this may result, and generally does result, from overwork, from worry, from dulness of life, inducing depression, from lack of rest, or from living or working amid unhealthy surroundings. Hence you will find many professional men give way to drink from sheer mental over-strain, and you will find many dwellers in the slums give way to drink from loss of sleep, from over-work, from ill-health, or from the effects of foul air.

Or a man may become a drunkard from the habit of taking drink. Doubtless there are many thousands of men working in the coal mines, or iron works, or as coal dischargers, or as wool staplers, or masons, or chemical labourers, who from the intense heat, or severe exertion, or choking dust, amongst which they labour are compelled to drink freely, and so acquire the morbid taste for liquor.

Or a man may lead a dull and cheerless life, and live amid squalid and gloomy surroundings, and so may contract the habit of going to the public-house for company and change and for excitement, and so may acquire the habit of drinking by those means.

Or a man may have inherited the disease from drunken parents; parents who acquired it from one of the causes above-named.

Now, Mr. Smith, you know that many of the poor work at unhealthy trades and live in

unhealthy places; and you know that they work too hard and too long, and that their lives are dull and anxious, and I ask you is it surprising that such people take to drink?

Moreover, those purists who bear so hardly upon the workers for this fault, have seldom a word to say against the men who drive them to drink. But the real culprits, the people actually responsible for nearly all the drunkenness of the poor, are the grasping employers, the polluters of the rivers and the air, the jerry-builders, the slum-lords, and the detestable knaves who grow rich by the sale of poisoned and adulterated liquor.

Give the people healthy homes, human lives, due leisure and amusement, and pure meat and drink, and drunkenness will soon disappear. While there are slums, while men have no pure pleasure, while they are overworked, and untaught, and while the wealthy brewer can open his poison dens at every street corner, it will be useless to preach temperance. The late Dean of Manchester spoke like a man of sense when he said that if he lived in the slums he too would take to drink.

Do you doubt me when I say that it is the surroundings that make the vices of the people?

Put a number of well-disposed people into bad surroundings and compel them to stop there. In a century you will have the kind of people now to be found in the slums. Take, now, a lot of people from the slums and put them in a new country where they must work to live, where they can live by work, where fresh air and freedom and hope can come to them, and in a generation you will have a prosperous and creditable colony. Do you not know this to be true? Has it not happened both ways? Do not Dr. Barnardo's outcast children turn out well? Then what is the reason? Men are made by their environment.

It has been said that dirt is matter in the wrong place. I often think that ne'er-do-wells are examples of energy in the wrong place. Emerson says "There is no moral deformity but is a good passion out of place." Some natures cannot thrive without a great deal of excitement. They have in them such desire of activity, such hunger for adventure, that they are incapable of settling down to the dull humdrum life of British respectability and profit-making. Sir Walter Raleigh was a bold explorer and a grand admiral, but I cannot imagine him a success as a Lancashire weaver, with £1 a week and two holidays a year. Turn these restless spirits loose in a congenial sphere, and they will do much good work, as, indeed, much good work has been done by such. But dulness and monotony, task work and tracts, are not food hot enough for their palates. And so they seek such change and such excitement as lie in their way. And the dealer in doctored gin and the retailer of racing " morals " find their profit in them; but they *might* have been fine factors in the sum of human progress.

To tell these people that they shall have help and love when they quit their vices is like telling a sick man that he shall be sent to the sea-side as soon as he recovers his health.

Sow some wheat on sterile land, and it will give a poor harvest. Would you say, " While there are poor harvests there must be sterile lands?" Put a fish into a small and dirty globe, and he will sicken. Would you say that while there are sick fishes there must be small globes and impure water? Yet you say while there are vice and improvidence there must be poverty.

Why do the middle and upper classes take so much trouble with the nursing and education of their children? Why do they instil into their young minds principles of honesty, of industry, of virtue, of culture? Why do they send their sons and daughters to school and to college? Why do they teach them cleanliness and sobriety? Why do they so jealously watch over their morals? Why do they take such trouble and incur such expense in the effort to shield them from all that is vicious, and indecent, and unhealthy? Is it not to ensure their moral and mental and physical welfare? You will say, " Of course."

It seems, then, that even the children of educated, honest, and virtuous parents need to be carefully trained and guarded to prevent them falling into idleness and vice. For if children would grow up good without watchfulness and cultivation, it would be mere folly

and waste of time and means to trouble about teaching them. Now if all this care is necessary to ensure moral excellence, it follows that without such care moral excellence could not be ensured. That is to say, that in our colleges, in our Sunday schools, in our home lessons, in the tender and earnest solicitude of good parents, we find an acknowledgment of the fact that a child is what he is taught to be.

Now suppose a child is deprived of this education. Suppose it is born in a poor hovel, in a poor slum. Suppose its home surroundings are such that cleanliness and modesty are well-nigh impossible. Suppose the gutter is its playground; the gin-shop its nursery; the factory its college; the drunkard its exemplar; the ruffian and the thief its instructors! Suppose bad nursing, bad air, bad water, bad food, dirt, hunger, ill-usage, foul language, and hard work are its daily portion. Suppose it has inherited poor blood, dull spirits, enfeebled wits, and stunted stature, from its ill-fed, untaught, overworked, miserable, ignorant, and unhealthy parents, can you expect that child to be clever, and moral, and thrifty, and clean, and sober?

Again. What next to their education and surroundings makes well-bred and well-taught children happy and good and industrious? Simply their good and pleasant environment. Life is to them worth living. They have comfort and love and knowledge and—hope. But the child of " the great unwashed " has none of these things. His lot is labour and poverty, his pleasure is in drunkenness and gambling, his future is gloomier than his horrible present. You talk about the social virtues! These poor creatures have not even food, or rest, or air, or light! Now, I say, give them food and air, and light and leisure; give them education and give them hope, and they will cease to be vicious and improvident.

The poor! The poor! The poor! The thriftlessness of the poor! The intemperance of the poor! The idleness of the poor! How long yet have we to listen to this cackle? How long have we to hear men prate about the poor and about the working classes who never knew what poverty is, who never knew what hunger means, who never did a stroke of manual work, and whose knowledge of "the poor" is got from the poems and the novels and the essays of university "swells," or from furtive and uncharitable glances at the public-house steps or the pawnshop door as their excellencies' carriages are hurrying them through the outskirts of the slums!

Perhaps you will say, John, that if the surroundings make the man, then all the denizens of the slums, and all the workers in the mines, would drink. But, no. You would not say that the bad drainage of a district would give all the inhabitants the fever, but only that it would give those the fever whose health made them most amenable to the germs of the disease.

I am not arguing that poverty inevitably leads to drink, but only that it is the chief cause of drunkenness.

There is a common belief to the effect that if the poor were all industrious, sober, and thrifty they would cease to be poor. This error arises from confusion of thought.

It is quite true that a sober man will succeed better than a drunken man; but it is not true that if all the people were sober their wages would increase.

Suppose there are ten clerks in an office, nine of whom are unsteady and one steady. The steady man will very likely become head clerk. But this is not because he is steady, but because the others are not steady. For you will observe that no one thinks of promoting a clerk because he is honest, for very few clerks being dishonest the honest clerk is not singular.

You must not suppose that because a sober and industrious *man* will succeed—in *some* trades—better than a drunken and a lazy man that therefore the whole trade would succeed better by becoming abstainers and hard workers.

You are fond of "facts," Mr. Smith. What are the facts with regard to thrift and industry amongst the workers?

The Hindoos are amongst the most abstemious and industrious people; and they are about the worst-paid people in the world. The immigrant Jews in the tailoring and slipper trades are wonderfully thrifty, sober, and industrious, and they work terribly long hours for shamefully low wages.

Under competition the workers do not gain any advantage by being sober and industrious. They gain a lower depth of serfdom and a harder task of slavery. If the Englishman will work for fifteen hours and live on bread and cheese, the foreigner will have to work for eighteen hours and eat grass, and *that* is what your capitalists mean when they tell you that Englishmen are being pushed out of the market by foreigners because foreigners will work harder and take less pay.

But allow me to quote the statement of this case given by me in my reply to the Bishop of Manchester:—

"In all foreign nations where the standard of living is lower than in England, your lordship will find that the wages are lower also.

"Has not your lordship often heard our manufacturers tell the English workers that if they would emulate the thrift and sobriety of the foreigner they might successfully compete against foreign competition in the foreign markets? My lord, what does that mean, but that thrift would enable our people to live on less, and so to accept less wages?

"Your lordship knows that our shirtmakers here in Manchester are miserably paid.

"This is because capitalism always keeps the wages down to the lowest standard of subsistence which the people will accept.

"So long as our English women will consent to work long hours, and live on tea and bread, the 'law of supply and demand' will maintain the present condition of sweating in the shirt trade.

"If all our women became firmly convinced that they could not exist without chops and bottled stout the wages *must* go up to a price to pay for those things.

"*Because there would be no women offering to live on tea and bread;* and shirts *must* be had.

"But what, my lord, is the result of the abstinence of these poor sisters of ours? Low wages for themselves, and, for others—— ?

"A young merchant wants a dozen shirts. He pays 10s. each for them. He meets a friend who only gave 8s. for his. He goes to the 8s. shop and saves 24s. This is clear profit, and he spends it in cigars, or champagne, or in some other luxury; *and the poor seamstress lives on toast and tea.*"

Many shallow thinkers assert that if a man is determined to succeed he *will* succeed. This is not true, but if it were true it would not prove that the qualities of energy, talent, and self-denial which enable one man to improve his condition would enable all men to improve their conditions. For the one man only succeeds because of his superior strength or skill; but if all men displayed strength and skill equal to his he could not rise.

There is a panic in a theatre and a fight for egress. A big strong man will force his way out over the bodies of the weak.

Now don't you see how foolish it is for that man to tell the weak that if they were as strong as he *they* could get out? If they were as strong as he, he could not get out himself.

A short time ago a certain writer, much esteemed for his graceful style of saying silly things, informed us that the poor remain poor because they show no efficient desire to be anything else. Is that true, John Smith? Are only the idle poor? Come with me and I will show you where men and women work from

morning till night, from week to week, from year to year, at the full stretch of their powers, in dim and fœtid dens, and yet are poor—ay, destitute—have for their wages a crust of bread and rags. I will show you where men work in dirt and heat, using the strength of brutes, for a dozen hours a day, and sleep at night in styes, until brain and muscle are exhausted, and fresh slaves are yoked to the golden car of commerce, and the broken drudges filter through the union or the prison to a felon's or a pauper's grave! And I will show you how men and women thus work and suffer and faint and die, generation after generation; and I will show you how the longer and the harder these wretches toil the worse their lot becomes; and I will show you the graves, and find witnesses to the histories of brave and noble and industrious poor men whose lives were lives of toil *and* poverty, and whose deaths were tragedies.

And all these things are due to *sin*—but it is to the sin of the smug hypocrites who grow rich upon the robbery and the ruin of their fellow-creatures.

CHAPTER XXII.

YOU have very likely heard, Mr. Smith, of the thing called Individualism. You may have read articles or heard speeches in which Socialism has been assailed as an interference with the rights of the individual. You may have wondered why, among the rights of the individual, no place was given to the right to live; or that the apostles of Individualism should be so strangely blind to the danger of leaving private enterprise un-curbed. But you need not wonder about these things, for Individualism is a relic of savagery, and its apologists would be agitating for the return of the good old individual right of carrying a stone club and living by promiscuous robbery and murder, were they not convinced that the law of supply and demand, although a more cowardly and brutal weapon than the cannibal's club, is infinitely more deadly and effective.

Society consists of individuals—so Herbert

Spencer says. And that dogma, if it means anything, means that society is a concourse of independent atoms, and not a united whole. But you know that statement is not in accord with fact or reason—not to speak of morality. You know that society consists of a number of more or less antagonistic parties, united amongst themselves for purposes of social warfare, and that where an independent individual is found he is always either a good man, trying to persuade the combatants to reason and righteousness; or a bad man, trying to fleece them that his own nest may be warm.

How, indeed, can society be a multitude of unconnected units? I look in my dictionary, and I find the word "society" defined as "a union of persons in one interest; fellowship." And clearly a society means a number of men joined by interest or affection. For how can that be a society which has no social connections? A mob of antagonistic individuals is a chaos, not a society.

And with regard to that claim that men should be left free to fight each for his own hand—is that civilisation or anarchy? And will it result in peace or in war, in prosperity or in disaster? Not civilisation, John, but savagery; not Christianity, but cannibalism is the spirit of this doctrine of selfishness and folly. And I ask you again in this case, as I did in the case of the gospel of "avarice": Is not love stronger than hate? And will not a society founded on love and justice certainly flourish, as the society founded on hate and strife will certainly perish?

Before you answer look around you at the state of England to-day, and cast back in your mind for the lessons of the nations that are gone. What is the apex of the gospel of avarice and of the law of supply and demand? Sweating! What is the result of the liberty of the individual to cozen the strong and destroy the weak for the sake of useless gain or worthless power? Does not one man wax rich by making many poor—one man dwell in a palace by keeping many in hovels? And are not the people crushed with taxation, which the impotent and lazy squander and misuse?

One Individualist, Mr. Levy, in an article written by him against Socialism a few years ago, says that—

The Individualist denies to A and B the right of prescribing for C what will do him good, and forcing it down his throat by the aid of the policeman's truncheon. He denies that A and B have any right whatever to coerce C, *except to prevent him invading the rights of others, and to exact from him his share in the maintenance of the common liberties.*

The italics are mine. On this point we are agreed. Our difference is as to what constitutes an "Invasion of the rights of others." I say, why punish the kind of thief we call a burglar, and not the kind of thief we call a sweater? Why hang the murderer who kills in the heat of passion and from motives of jealousy or revenge, and not the murderer who slays wholesale by the death-trap of the slums, and slays in cold blood, and from the bestial motive of gain?

Mr. Levy says of Individualism:—

It would strive to make the law such that, in the words of Kant—"Every one may seek his own happiness in the way that seems good to himself, provided that he infringe not such freedom of others to strive after a similar end as is consistent with the freedom of all."

This is the same idea expressed in different words. Where are we to draw the line as to the "infringement of the freedom of others?" Are we to let the sweater and the retailer of diseased meat "seek their own happiness in a way that seems good to themselves"? Are we to stop the men who infringe the freedom of others by aid of the machinery of capitalist monopoly? Or are we only to stop the other rogues and ruffians who infringe our freedom with the bludgeon and the bullet? We agree that it is right for society to protect itself against *some* scoundrels. We differ as to which scoundrels are to be restrained.

Mr. Auberon Herbert says:—

Government has no moral right to compel men for their own good, but only to restrain them from such aggressions upon each other as involve physical force, or such direct fraud as is the equivalent of physical force, from the point of view of the consent to transaction of the defrauded person.

And another tract of his is headed by the following quotation from Mr. Herbert Spencer:—

The liberty of each, limited alone by the like liberty of all.

Now, you'll observe that Government is here granted the power to restrain one man from injuring another by physical violence, or from injuring him by "direct fraud," but is not to have power to restrain the operations of indirect fraud. But why should Government be allowed to prevent violence? Why should Government be allowed to prevent murder or highway robbery? I don't know what reason the Individualist has for his belief that Government should defend the subject from the burglar and the forger. Because, if it is best to let the more criminal and more dangerous sweater rob and slay, I cannot understand why it is necessary to interfere with the footpad and the scuttler. The reason I have for supporting the Government in its protection of the subject is easily given. But I'd rather use the word Society than the word Government.

Society, according to my philosophy, is a union of people for mutual advantage. Every member of a society must give up some small fraction of his own will and advantage in return for the advantages he gains by association with his fellows. One of the advantages he derives from association with his fellows is protection from injury. The chief function of Government—which is the executive power of the society's will—is to protect the subject. Against whom is the subject to be protected? I should say against foreign enemies, against injury by his fellow-subjects, and against calamities caused by his own ignorance. We will lay by the first and third propositions, and consider the second.

The subject is to be protected by the Government from injury by his fellow-subjects. Here I traverse the position of the Individualists. They will restrain the assassin and the passer of base coin, but they will not suffer any interference with the sacred liberty of the slum landlord or the sweater. And I fail to see their reason.

There is no reason visible to my mind for empowering the Government, or society, to hang the man who steals a watch and murders the owner, except the reason I have given—that it is for the general advantage that society should be allowed to protect one of its members from injury by another. If that is the real reason why Government may hang a Charles Peace or send an "Artful Dodger" to gaol, then it is also a sufficient reason why Government protection should be extended beyond the limits laid down in Mr. Herbert's tracts. Because the sweater, and the rack-renter, and the respectable dealer in adulterated goods are not only morally worse than the footpad and the area-sneak, but they are also guilty of greater and more deadly injury to their fellow-subjects.

True, sweating and land-grabbing and other forms of the basest villainy are not illegal; and I would not have them illegally meddled with. But I would alter the law so that they should be illegal. This, I presume, Mr. Herbert would not do. He will only defend us from the garrotter and the confidence-trick man. But I think it is as bad for a railway company to work a man a hundred and eight hours for seventeen shillings, or for a landlord to charge rent for a death trap, or for a tailor to grind his hands down to a slavery that takes up all their waking hours and gives them in return a diet of bread and coffee, as for a thief to come and steal your false teeth. Nay, the sweater is altogether a more hateful, dangerous, deadly, and cowardly scoundrel than the pickpocket.

Of course, the sweater's slave and the railway porter are the "free" parties to the bargain. They need not accept the bloodsucker's terms unless they choose. They have an alternative—they can starve. But I presume that even the most confirmed Individualist would stop a man from jumping down a precipice, or throwing himself under a train. That would be physical injury, against which it is right to protect each other. But the poor girl who takes her suicide in the form of shirt-making is not to be interfered with. You must respect free contract and the liberty of the individual.

Individual liberty is what we all desire—so far as it is possible to have it. But it is *not* possible to have it in its complete form, whilst we live in communities. By living in communities, men get many advantages. It is not good for man to be alone. For the advantages that society gives us, we must make some sacrifice. We might well have much more individual liberty than we now have. We might easily have too much. We *have* too much—and too little—as things stand. A state of Socialism would give us all as much liberty as we need. A state of Individualism—of anarchy—would give *some* of us more liberty than it is wise and beneficial we should have.

Most men are honest, most men love justice. For the great mass of the people the law is almost a dead letter. Honest men need no laws—*except* to defend them from rascals. Have you ever asked yourselves, my friends, what price our rascals cost us? For *them* is all the costly machinery of Government, of armies, of fleets, of law courts, of prisons, police, workhouses, and the like maintained. Honest men do not need watching, for they would not steal; do not need repelling, for they would not invade. Consider the cost of all our police in its various forms, and then say what do our rascals cost us.

If it had not been for interference with the liberty of the individual and the freedom of contract in the past the lot of the workers would have been unbearable.

Do you know anything about the Truck Act, which abolished the nefarious custom of paying wages in bad food? Did you ever consider the effect of forbidding the payment of wages in public-houses, or the employment of climbing-boys by sweeps? Have you ever read the history of the Factory Acts? In "The Industrial History of England," by H. de B. Gibbins, M.A., you will find a few brief sketches of the state of things to which unchecked freedom of contract had reduced the factory workers before the Factory Acts were passed. From that book I will make a few extracts :—

ENGLISH SLAVERY: THE APPRENTICE SYSTEM.

It was not until the wages of the workmen had been reduced to a starvation level that they consented to their children and wives being employed in the mills. But the manufacturers wanted labour by some means or other, and they got it. They got it from the workhouses. They sent for parish apprentices from all parts of England, and pretended to apprentice them to the new employments just introduced. The mill-owners systematically communicated with the overseers of the poor, who arranged a day for the inspection of pauper children. Those chosen by the manufacturer were then conveyed by waggons or canal boats to their destination, and from that moment were doomed to slavery. Sometimes regular traffickers would take the place of the manufacturer, and transfer a number of children to a factory district, and there keep them, generally in some dark cellar, till they could hand them over to a mill-owner in want of hands, who would come and examine their height, strength, and bodily capacities, exactly as did the slave dealers in the American markets. After that the children were simply at the mercy of their owners, nominally as apprentices, but in reality as mere slaves, who got no wages, and whom it was not worth while to feed and clothe properly, because they were so cheap and their places could be so easily supplied. It was often arranged by the parish authorities, in order to get rid of imbeciles, that one idiot should be taken by the mill-owner with every twenty sane children. The fate of these unhappy idiots was even worse than that of the others. The secret of their final end has never been disclosed, but we can form some idea of their awful sufferings from the hardships of the other victims to capitalist greed and cruelty. Their treatment was most inhuman. The hours of their labour were only limited by exhaustion after many modes of torture had been unavailingly applied to force continued work. Children were often worked sixteen hours a day, by day and by night. Even Sunday was used as a convenient time to clean the machinery. The author of the "History of the Factory Movement" writes:—"In stench, in heated rooms, amidst the constant whirling of a thousand wheels, little fingers and little feet were kept in ceaseless action, forced into unnatural activity by blows from the heavy hands and feet of the merciless over-looker, and the infliction of bodily pain by instruments of punishment invented by the sharpened ingenuity of insatiable selfishness." They were fed upon the coarsest and cheapest food, often with the same as that served out to the pigs of their master. They slept by turns and in relays, in filthy beds which were never cool; one set of children were sent to sleep in them as soon as the others had gone off to their daily or nightly toil. There was often no discrimination of sexes; and disease and misery and vice grew as in a hot-bed of contagion. Some of these miserable beings tried to run away. To prevent their doing so those suspected of this tendency had irons riveted on their ankles with long links reaching to the hips, and were compelled to work and sleep in these chains, young women and girls as well as boys suffering this brutal treatment. Many died and were buried secretly at night in some desolate spot, lest people should notice the number of the graves; and many committed suicide.

In 1873, Lord Shaftesbury, speaking in the House of Lords, said :—

Well can I recollect, in the earlier periods of the factory movement, waiting at the factory gates to see the children come out, and a set of sad, dejected, cadaverous creatures they were. In Bradford, especially, the proofs of long and cruel toil were most remarkable. The cripples and distorted forms might be numbered by hundreds, perhaps by thousands. A friend of mine collected a vast number together for me; the sight was most piteous, the deformities incredible. They seemed to me, such were their crooked shapes, like a mass of crooked alphabets.

You will find further particulars of these horrors, Mr. Smith, in the Blue Books of the period. Read them; read also the Blue Books on the sweating system, and the reports of the Labour Commission; read the facts relating to the Truck Acts and the chain and nail trades, and then read Mrs. Browning's pathetic poem of "The Cry of the Children," and I think you will be cured of any lingering affection for the "Freedom of Contract" and the "Rights of the Individual."

I quite understand Mr. Herbert's desire for "Liberty." But we cannot have liberty while we have rascals. Liberty is another of the things we have to pay for the pleasure of the rascal's company. Now I think Individualism strengthens the hands of the rogue in his fight with the true man; and I think Socialism would fortify the true men against the rascals. I grant you that State Socialism would imply some interference with the liberty of the individual. But *which* individual? The scoundrel. Imagine a dozen men at sea in a boat with only two days' provisions. Would it be wise to consider the liberty of the individual? If the strongest man took all the food and left the others to starve would it be right or wrong for the eleven men to combine to bind him and divide all fairly? To let the strong or the cunning rob the weak or honest is Individualism. To prevent the rascal from taking what is not his own is Socialism.

CHAPTER XXIII.

IN this chapter, Mr. Smith, I shall deal with the subject of luxury, and shall endeavour to make clear to you the fact that the luxury of the rich is a direct cause of the misery of the poor.

It is very important that you should understand this matter, for it has been often and grossly confused by the statements of foolish or dishonest men.

It was held for a long time that the rich man in spending his money conferred a benefit upon the poor.

This error has long since been abandoned even by most political economists, and is now only uttered by writers in the Press, a class of men mostly ignorant and dishonest, and almost entirely stupid.

From Pressmen, writing for large daily papers, I quote three statements, all false and all foolish.

The first is that "the luxury of the rich finds useful employment for the poor."

The second that " the expenditure of the rich confers upon the poor the two great blessings of work and wages."

The third that " a rich man cannot spend his money without finding employment for vast numbers of people who without him must starve."

These statements, you will see, all amount to the same thing. The intelligent Pressmen who uttered them supposed that the rich man spent his own money, whereas he really spends the money of other people; that he found useful work for a number of men, whereas it is impossible to find a man useful work in making useless things; and that the men employed by the rich must starve were it not for his help, whereas if it were not for his

hindrance they would all be doing useful instead of useless work.

All the things made or used by man may be divided into two classes, under the heads of necessaries and luxuries.

I should include under the head of necessaries all those things which are necessary to the highest form of human life.

All those things which are not necessary to the highest form of human life I should call luxuries, or superfluities.

For instance, I should call food, clothing, houses, fuel, books, pictures, and musical instruments necessaries ; and I should call diamond ear-rings, race-horses, and broughams luxuries.

Now, it is evident that all those things, whether luxuries or necessaries, are made by labour. Diamond rings, loaves of bread, grand pianos, and flat irons, do not grow on trees. They must be made by the labour of the people, and it is very clear that the more luxuries a people produce the fewer necessaries they will produce.

If a community consists of ten thousand people, and if nine thousand people are making bread and one thousand are making jewellery, it is evident that there will be more bread than jewellery.

If in the same community nine thousand make jewellery and only one thousand make bread, there will be more jewellery than bread.

In the first case there will be food enough for all, though jewels be scarce. In the second case the people must starve, although they wear diamond rings on all their fingers.

In a well-ordered state no luxuries would be produced until there were enough necessaries for all.

Robinson Crusoe's first care was to secure food and shelter. Had he neglected his goats and his raisins and spent his time in making shell-boxes he would have starved. Under those circumstances he would have been a fool. But what are we to call the delicate and refined ladies who wear satin and pearls, while the people who earn them lack bread?

Take a community of two men. They work upon a plot of land and grow grain for food. By each working six hours a day they produce enough food for both.

Now take one of those men away from the cultivation of the land and set him to work for six hours a day at the making of bead necklaces. What happens?

This happens—that the man who is left upon the land must now work twelve hours a day. Why? Because, although his companion has ceased to grow grain he has not ceased to *eat bread*. Therefore the man who grows the grain must now grow grain enough for two. That is to say that the more men are set to the making of luxuries, the heavier will be the burden of the men who produce necessaries.

But in this case you see the farmer does get some return for his extra labour. That is to say, he gets half the necklaces in exchange for half his grain; for there is no rich man.

Suppose next a community of three—one of whom is a landlord, while the other two are farmers.

The landlord takes half the produce of the land in rent, but does no work. What happens?

We saw just now that the two workers could produce enough grain in six hours to feed two men for one day. Of this the landlord takes half. Therefore the two men must now produce four men's food in one day, of which the landlord will take two, leaving the workers each one. Well, if it takes a man six hours to produce a day's keep for one, it will take him twelve hours to produce a day's keep for two. So that our two farmers must now work twice as long as before.

But now the landlord has got twice as much grain as he can eat. He therefore proceeds to *spend* it, and in spending it he " finds useful employment " for one of the farmers. That is to say, he takes away one of the farmers off

the land and sets him to building a house for the landlord. What is the effect of this?

The effect of it is that the one man left upon the land has now to find food for all three, and in return gets nothing.

Consider this carefully. All men must eat, and here are two men who do not produce food. To produce food for one man takes one man six hours. To produce food for three men takes one man eighteen hours. The one man left on the land has therefore to work three times as long, or three times as hard as he did at first. In the case of the two men we saw that the farmer did get his share of the bead necklaces, but in the case of the three men the farmer gets nothing. The luxuries produced by the man taken from the land are enjoyed by the rich man.

The landlord takes from the farmer two-thirds of his produce, and employs another man to help him to spend it.

We have here three classes:—

1. The landlord who does no work.

2. The landlord's servant who does work for the benefit of the landlord.

3. The farmer who produces food for himself and the other two.

Now, all the peoples of Europe, if not of the world, are divided into those three classes.

In my lecture on luxury I showed these things by diagrams. We will use a diagram representing a community of ten men supporting a figure representing ten men's food. Thus:—

TEN MEN'S FOOD.

✳✳✳✳✳✳✳✳✳✳

All the men represented here by stars are employed in making necessaries, and the figure they support is the amount of their labour.

Now what I want you to clearly understand is that although you take away one of those ten men and set him to other work you do not take him away from the consumption of food. He has still to be fed, and he must be fed by the men who produce food. Suppose, then, that we take away seven of our ten men; that we make one of them a Chief, and six of them the Chief's servants, the figure will be left thus:

TEN MEN'S FOOD.

✳✳✳

The burden is the same, *ten men's food* ; but the bearers are fewer.

C is a jeweller, and sets diamonds for B. Where does B get the money to pay him? he gets the money from A. It is clear then that A is keeping both B and C.

Now we are told upon the authority of Mulhall and Giffen—see Fabian tract, "Facts for Socialists," price one penny—that the division of the national earnings is as follows :—

	Millions.
Rent	200
Interest	250
Salaries & profits of middle-class	350
Wages of workers	450
	1,250

The population is about 36 millions. The annual income about 1,250 million pounds. One-third of the people take two-thirds of the wealth, and the other two-thirds of the people take one-third of the wealth.

That is to say that 24 millions of workers produce 1,250 millions of wealth and give 800 millions of it to 12 millions of idlers and non-producers.

This means that each worker works one-third of his time for himself, and two-thirds of his time for other people.

This looks bad enough, but it is not the worst. Amongst the 24 millions of the working classes there are vast numbers of non-producers. There are millions of children and of women who produce nothing, and there must be millions of male " workers " who are engaged in producing superfluities. Canon Girdlestone, in his pamphlet, " Society Classified," says :—

It has been shown (by Alexander Wylie, in his "Labour, Leisure, and Luxury ") that, even if we give a liberal extension of meaning to the terms " necessaries " and " comforts " of life, so large a proportion as four-elevenths of the entire working population of this country are engaged in producing what, in contradistinction to the above, must properly be classified as " luxuries," *i.e.*, commodities, &c., such as to healthy minds in healthy bodies are the merest superfluities. And if, as probably is the case, most of these embodiments of the " services " (or, as Dr. Thring calls them, " the stored-up life ") of others are purchased by " non-workers," and paid for in "money" only, the bad effect of the transaction taken as a whole cannot be trifling or contemptible!

I should very much like to see society classi-fied. If it were classified, and the number producing necessaries and the number producing luxuries were clearly shown, I think we should find that every adult male now engaged in producing necessaries is supporting about twenty people.

My Lady Dedlock "finds useful employment" for Crispin, the shoe-maker. She employs him to make court slippers for her. Let us examine this transaction.

First, where does my lady get her money ? She gets it from her husband, Sir Leicester Dedlock, who gets it from his tenant farmer, who gets it from the agricultural labourer, Hodge.

Then she employs Crispin to make Court slippers, and pays him with Hodge's money.

But if Crispin were not employed in making shoes for my Lady he would be making boots for Hodge, or for the children of Hodge.

Whereas, now, Hodge cannot buy boots because he has no money, and he has no money because my Lady Dedlock has taken it.

Or my Lady orders a silk ball dress from Mrs. Mantilini. For this also she pays with money earned by Hodge, and meanwhile what kind of an old rag is worn by Mrs. Hodge?

Again, as bearing on this question of my Lady Dedlock's finding useful labour. I quote from a letter on the " Scarcity of Dairymaids," in the *Pall Mall Gazette.* Dairymaids are wanted, and dairymaids cannot be found. Then again a northern factor says in *The North British Agriculturalist* that he cannot get dairy-maids—though he offers £22 a year and board. The writer in the *Pall Mall* asks :—

What would the "Special Commissioner" say about " Life in our Villages" if the £10,000,000 we paid last year for foreign butter, the £4,000,000 for cheese, the £4,000,000 for margarine, and the £4,000,000 for eggs had been kept at home, giving employment to thousands—tens and hundreds of thousands—of our own countrymen and women, instead of foreigners?

Don't you think it would be an improvement if some of the " usefully " employed domestic servants and milliners, weavers, spinners, and flower girls in the pay of Lady Dedlock were set to work to save the £22,000,000 spent on foreign dairy produce, because there are no hands here to produce these needed things ?

What a lot of foggy thinkers there are in the world to be sure. Just look for a moment at this pamphlet. It is called " The Functions of Wealth," and is by W. H. Mallock. Here is a pretty sentence :—

That wealth, which is envied by so many, and which is looked upon doubtfully by so many more, so far from being the cause of want amongst thousands, is at this moment the cause of the non-starvation of millions.

Which means that it is the rich man who keeps the working poor, and not the working poor who keep the idle rich.

Mr. Mallock, in another place—he is explaining that it is an error to think one man's wealth is another's want—says :—

Let us take, for instance, a large and beautiful cabinet, for which a rich man of taste pays two thousand pounds. The cabinet is of value to him, for reasons which we will consider presently; as possessed by him it constitutes a portion of his wealth. But how could such a piece of wealth be distributed ? Not only is it incapable of physical partition and distribution, but, if taken from the rich man and given to the poor man, the latter is not the least enriched by it. Put a priceless buhl cabinet into an Irish labourer's cottage, and it will probably only add to his discomforts ; or, if he finds it useful it will only be because he keeps his pigs in it. A picture by Titian, again, may be worth thousands, but it is worth thousands only to the man who can enjoy it.

Now, isn't that a precious piece of cackle ? There are two things to be said about that rich man's cabinet. The first is that it was made by some workman who, if he had not been so employed, might have been producing what *would* be useful to the poor. So that the cabinet has cost the poor something. The second is that a priceless buhl cabinet *can* be divided. Of course, it would be folly to hack it into shavings and serve them out amongst the mob ; but if that cabinet is a thing of beauty and worth the seeing, it ought to be taken from the rich benefactor, whose benefaction consists in his having plundered it from the poor, and it ought to be put into a public museum where thousands could see it, and where the rich man could see it also if he chose. This, indeed, is the proper way to deal with all works of art, and this is one of the rich man's greatest crimes—that he keeps hoarded up in his house a number of things that ought to be the common heritage of the people.

Every article of luxury has to be paid for not in *money* but in *labour.* Every glass of wine drunk by my lord, and every diamond star worn by my lady, has to be paid for with the sweat and the tears of the poorest of our people. I believe it is a literal fact that many of the artificial flowers worn at court, are actually stained with the tears of the famished and exhausted girls who make them.

It is often asserted that the Capitalist is as necessary to the Labourer as the Labourer is to the Capitalist, and we are asked, therefore,

How are we going to do without the Capitalist?

This question is based upon a confusion of thought as to the meanings of the two terms, Capital and Capitalist.

The Pope in his Encyclical falls into this muddle. He states the Labour Question as " The problem of how to adjust the respective claims of capital and labour."

But to talk about the respective claims of capital and labour is as absurd as to talk about the respective claims of coal and colliers, or engines and engine-drivers.

There is a vast difference between capital and the capitalist. Capital is necessary ; but capitalists are not necessary.

What do we mean by the word capital? There are many definitions of the word. But it will suffice for us to say that capital means the material used in the production and distribution of wealth. That is to say, under the term capital we include land, factories, canals, railways, machinery, and money.

But the capitalist is not capital. He is the person who owns capital. He is the person who lends capital. He is the person who charges interest for the use of capital.

This " capital " which he lends at usury ! *He* did not produce it. *He* does not use it. He only *charges* for it.

Who *did* produce the capital ? *All* capital is produced by labour. Who *does* use the capital ? Capital cannot be used except by labour.

To say that we could not work without capital is as true as to say that we could not mow without a scythe. To say that we could not work without a capitalist is as false as to say that we could not mow a meadow unless all the scythes belonged to one man. Nay, it is as false as to say that we could not mow unless all the scythes belonged to one man and *he* took a third of the harvest as payment for the loan of them.

Instances: There is valuable capital in the British Telegraphs; but there is no capitalist. The telegraph is a Socialistic institution. The State draws the revenues *from the people*, and the State administers the work. In our State Departments, and Municipal Departments, there is much capital, but there are no capitalists. The manager of a mine is necessary, the owner of a mine is not necessary ; the captain of a ship is useful, the owner of a ship is useless.

These are undeniable *proofs*, as are the roads we walk on, and the lamps that light our way, that " capital " and " capitalist " are *not* convertible terms.

Mr. Hart, in his pamphlet on Constitutional Socialism, puts the case against the capitalist very clearly. He says:—

The practicability of Socialism can nevertheless be demonstrated by the present practical working of huge institutions in commerce, industry, and agriculture, which are gradually ruining many smaller ones. These enterprises derive their capital either from a gigantic capitalist or from a lot of shareholders, who know nothing about the business themselves, and who simply pay managers and clerks or manual workers to do the work for them. Now, whether there are 8,000 of these shareholders in a country, or 80,000, or 8,000,000, that does not affect the question, which is: Can shareholders find managers to produce, transport, and sell wealth for them? Answer: Yes, as it is being done at present.

Moreover, if it is practical for these managers and their dependents to conduct business in a state of competition, with the risk of being ruined by the intrigues or inventions of their rivals, *a fortiori* would it be practical for such managers and dependents to conduct business when this risk no longer existed, and when they had simply to produce a certain number of goods, according to the demand, and then to transport these goods to shops or stores for sale ?

And so much for the question of how can Labour dispense with Capitalists.

One more question, and I may conclude this chapter :—

Will not the spread of Socialistic ideas tend to alarm the capitalist, and so cause him to take his capital out of the country ?

Take his capital out of the country ! He might take himself out of the country, and he would doubtless take all the portable property he could carry. But the country could bear the loss. Let me quote once more from John Stuart Mill :—

When men talk of the ancient wealth of a country,

of riches inherited from ancestors, and similar expressions, the idea suggested is, that the riches so transmitted were produced long ago, at the time when they are said to have been first acquired, and that no portion of the capital of a country was produced this year, except so much as may have been this year added to the total amount. The fact is far otherwise.

The greater part, in value, of the wealth now existing in England has been produced by human hands within the last twelve months. A very small proportion indeed of that large aggregate was in existence ten years ago ; of the present productive capital of the country scarcely any part, except farm houses and factories, and a few ships and machines, and even these would not in most cases have survived so long, if fresh labour had not been employed within that period in putting them into repair.

The land subsists, and the land is almost the only thing that subsists. Everything which is produced perishes, and most things very quickly.

Capital is kept in existence from age to age, not by preservation, but by perpetual reproduction.

This threat about the capitalist taking his capital out of the country is a common one. It is always used when workmen strike against a reduction of wages. It was used during the cotton strike, and during the coal strike.

Now just fancy the millowners and the coalowners taking their capital out of the country. They might take some of their machinery ; they could not take their mills, nor their mines. The threat is nonsense.

Imagine the landlords and capitalists, the shareholders and dividend-mongers, marching off with the farms, and fields, and streets ; the mills and mines ; the railways, and quarries, and canals.

No : let the capitalist go when he will ; he must leave England and the English behind him, and they will suffice for each other. It is the capitalist who keeps them apart, paralysing both, robbing both, and helping neither.

A more idiotic assumption was never made than this assumption that the wasting of wealth by the idle rich is a good thing for the labouring poor. Follow it out to its logical conclusion, John Smith, and assure yourself that the drunkard is a benefactor to the workers because he finds much " useful employment " for the coopers, hop - growers, maltsters, and others who are doomed to waste their time in the production of the *ir* c which slakes his swinish lust.

CHAPTER XXIV.

I N this chapter I propose to answer a few of those questions which are so often put to Socialist writers and lecturers.

1. Under Socialism: What will you do with your loafers?

Before I answer this question allow me to offer a few hints to young Socialists. The opponents of Socialism appear to suppose that if they can suggest any difficulty, however trivial, which may arise in the working of our system, they have disposed of the whole matter. Very many ardent but inexperienced young Socialists fall into the error of trying to prove that Socialism and Heaven are the same thing.

Both sides should remember that Socialism is not offered as a perfect system of life, but only as a very great improvement upon the system under which we now live.

The question, then, is not whether Socialism is the best thing man can conceive, but whether Socialism is better than our present method of life.

Therefore, when a critic asks a young Socialist whether a certain evil will exist under Socialism, let the Socialist immediately ask his critic whether the same evil exists *now*.

So in the case of the loafer. Many overconfident, but not very profound, critics demand triumphantly, " What will you do with your loafers?"

To them I say, " What do *you* do with your loafers?"

The word loafer, I take it, means one who loafs or sponges upon the earnings of other people.

A loafer, then, may be an idle tramp without a shirt to his back, or he may be an idle peer with a rent-roll of half a million a year.

It is stated in one of the Fabian tracts— " Facts for Socialists "—that there are something like a million of adult males in receipt of large incomes who never do any kind of work at all.

Under Socialism these men might continue idle; but they would certainly not continue rich, nor would they continue to be known as " gentlemen."

But besides the millions of well paid and well fed loafers who are at present supported upon the earnings of the poor, there are now in this country immense numbers of paupers, beggars, tramps, and criminals, as well as a large army of unemployed workers.

Now before I tell you what would be done with all these people under Socialism, I must tell you what is done with them now.

Do you suppose that society does not support these loafers? But they live; and what do they live on?

All wealth is won by labour, is it not? Then all the tramps, thieves, paupers, and beggars live upon poor-rates, plunder, alms, or prison allowances, and all these means of support are earned by the labour of the working poor.

But under your present system you not only feed and house these loafers, but you go to the expense of masters, matrons, doctors, warders, and police, all of whom have to be fed and paid to wait upon or attend to the loafers.

Next, with regard to the unemployed. These people exist; and they exist in enforced idleness, and at the expense of those who work.

Note one or two facts. These people do nothing for their own support, and many of them, through want and shame and forced idleness, become criminals or tramps.

This is not only a waste of wealth, and a waste of power, it is also a most wicked and disgraceful waste of human souls.

Now, let us see how things would work out under Socialism. We will divide our loafers into two classes. Those who could work and will not, and those who would work and cannot.

So long as it is possible for a willing worker to be forced into idleness, so long will there exist a reason for the giving of alms.

Why do we relieve a tramp on the road, or a

beggar in the street? It is because we are never sure that the man is a loafer; because we always fear that his penury may be due to misfortune, and not to idleness.

But under Socialism this doubt would disappear. Under Socialism there would be work for all. Therefore, under Socialism every man who was able to work would be able to live. This fact being universally known, no ablebodied man could exist without work. A beggar or a tramp would be inevitably a loafer, and not a hand would be held out to help him.

The answer to the able-bodied beggar would be, "If you are hungry go and work." If the man refused to work he must starve.

The answer, then, to the question of what Socialists would do with the loafers is, that under Socialism we should oblige the loafer to work or perish; whereas, under present conditions, we either make him into a "gentleman," or a pauper, or a beggar, or a thief; in any one of which capacities he is allowed to live in idleness upon the labour of other men.

Tell me, John Smith, is it not true of Merrie England to-day that the idlest are the richest, and the most industrious the poorest amongst the people? Well, I want you to remind your critics of these things when they ask you what Socialists will do with their loafers.

Let us take another question.

2. Under Socialism: Who will do the disagreeable work? *Who will do the scavenging?*

This question is an old friend of mine, and I have come to entertain for it a tender affection. I have seldom heard an argument or read an adverse letter or speech against the claims of justice in social matters, but our friend the scavenger played a prominent part therein. Truly, this scavenger is a most important person. Yet one would not suppose that the whole cosmic scheme revolved on him as on an axis; one would not imagine him to be the keystone of European society—at least, his appearance and his wages would not justify such an assumption. But I begin to believe that the fear of the scavenger is really the source and fountain head, the life and blood and breath of all conservatism. Good old scavenger. His ash-pan is the bulwark of

capitalism, and his besom the standard around which rally the pride and the culture and the opulence of British society. And he never knew it; he does not know it now. If he did he would strike for another penny a day.

We have heard a good deal of more or less clumsy ridicule at the expense of the Socialists. We have heard learned and practical men laugh them to scorn; we have seen their claims and their desires and their theories held up to derision. But can any man imagine a sight more contemptible or more preposterous than that of a civilised and wealthy nation coming to a halt in its march of progress for fear of disturbing the minds of the scavengers?

Shades of Cromwell, of Langton, of Washington, and of Hampden! Imagine the noble lord at the head of the British Government aweing a truculent and Radical Parliament into silence by thundering out the terrible menace, "Touch the dustmen, and you destroy the Empire." Yet, when the noble lord talks about "tampering with the laws of political economy," and "opening the floodgates of anarchy," it is really the scavenger that is in his mind, although the noble lord may not think so himself, noble lords not being always very clear in their reasonings. For just as Mrs. Partington sought to drive back the ocean with a mop, so does the Conservative hope to drive back the sea of progress with the scavenger's broom.

For an answer to this question I must refer you back to my chapter on Socialism and Slavery. But the whole subject has, I find, been very clearly and ably dealt with by Mrs. Besant in her excellent paper on "The Organisation of Society" in the Fabian Essays. Mrs. Besant says:—

There are unpleasant and indispensable forms of labour which, one would imagine, can attract none—mining, sewer-cleaning, &c. These might be rendered attractive by making the hours of labour in them much shorter than the normal working day of pleasanter occupations. . . . . .

Further, much of the most disagreeable and laborious work might be done by machinery, as it would be now if it were not cheaper to exploit a helot class. When it became illegal to send small boys up chimneys, chimneys did not cease to be swept; a machine was invented for sweeping them.

The same idea is expressed in Bellamy's "Looking Backward."

In the army the various duties are taken in turns. Guard duty, picquet duty, and the numerous laborious or unpleasant tasks known as "fatigue" are done by parties of men told off for the purpose, and no man can escape his share.

And how is this work done in Merrie England to-day? Clearly we all recognise that scavenging is unpleasant work. Clearly we all agree that no man would do it from choice. But some men do it, and the inference is that they do it on compulsion. They do it, and are made to work long hours for low wages, and are despised for their pains.

This is gross tyranny and gross injustice, but it is only another example of the meanness, the selfishness, and the dishonesty of those whom we falsely call the refined and superior classes. It is amusing to hear that a man is "too much of a gentleman" to empty his own ashpit, when the truth is that he is not enough of a gentleman to refuse to allow his fellow-citizen to empty it for him. Under Socialism snobbery will perish. And when snobbery is dead, gentility will be ready for burial.

Another common question is :—

3. Under Socialism : Would the frugal workman lose his house and savings ?

First, as to the savings. M. Richter, in his foolish pamphlet, "Pictures of the Future," makes the people revolt because a Socialistic Government has nationalised their savings.

Now, Mr. Smith, we will assume that such a thing happened, and that the deposits in the banks were nationalised. Would the frugal workman lose by that? I say he would not.

It is true that at present the frugal workman only gets about one-third of his earnings. Under Socialism he would get *all* his earnings.

But why does the frugal workman save? He saves against a "rainy day." Because if he fall ill, or live to be old and infirm, he will have to go to the workhouse unless he has saved.

But under Socialism he need have no fear. No man would be left destitute or helpless in his old age. The sick would be cared for, the widows and orphans would be cherished and defended.

You know that many men now pay high premiums to insurance companies. This is to provide for their widows and children. Under Socialism the State would provide for the widows and children.

That is to say that Socialism is the finest scheme of life insurance ever yet devised.

Suppose you had by dint of great care succeeded in saving two or three hundred pounds. Would you not cheerfully pay that for a State promise of support for yourself when old—of ample and honourable support—and of support and education for your children after your death ?

But I don't think it is at all likely that a Socialist State *would* take the worker's savings.

And again I ask you to turn your attention to the present system, under which *every* worker is robbed of two-thirds of all he earns.

Then as to the worker's cottage. Assuming that he has bought it with his savings, and assuming that the State nationalised it. What then ? A workman now buys a house that he and his children may be sure of a home.

Under Socialism *every* man would be sure of a home.

Once more consider our present system. A few men own their own houses. But the great bulk of the people cannot own a foot of land.

When I was in Ireland. I visited some "estates" upon the Galtee Hills. I saw farms which had been *made* by the "tenants." I saw places where the peasants had gone up into the bleak hills, where the limestone blocks lay thick and only a thin layer of sandy turf covered the rock, and had spent twenty years in *making the land.* They removed the boulders, they dug soil in the valleys, and carried it up the steeps in baskets ; they bought manure and lime and they built their own hovels out of mud and stones.

And then the estate and houses were the property of the landlord, and he raised their rents from 200 to 500 per cent.

And we are asked whether Socialism would rob the frugal worker of his home !

It is strange that men should attach importance to such trivial points as these ; but yet I believe that these small errors are a great hindrance to the spread of Socialism.

Here is another droll question:—

4. Under Socialism : Who would get the salmon, and who would get the redherrings ?

Let us follow the system I suggested, and reverse the question. Who gets the salmon and who gets the red-herrings now?

Is it not true that the salmon and all other delicacies are monopolised by the idle, whilst the coarse food falls to the lot of the worker?

Perhaps under Socialism the salmon might be eaten by those who catch it. At present it is not.

Or perhaps the dainties would be reserved for invalids and old people, or for delicate women and children.

But certainly we should not see a lot of big, fat, strong aldermen gorging turtle and champagne while frail girls worked sixteen hours a day on a diet of crusts and coffee.

It is quite possible that even under Socialism there might not be enough salmon and pineapple for all. But it is quite certain that there would be enough bread and beef and tea for all, which there certainly is not *now*.

And so much for that question; and, if you care to follow it out more fully, I must refer you to my answer to Richter's "Pictures of the Future."

CHAPTER XXV.

THE capitalist Press, probably because they cannot controvert the theory of Socialism, are in the habit of abusing Socialists. Socialist writers and Socialist speakers, and very often Trade Union leaders, are commonly described as "Paid Agitators;" and our Labour papers are charged with "pandering to the worst passions of the mob," and with "battening on the earnings of ignorant dupes."

This is pretty much the same kind of language as that which the Press employed against John Bright, Ernest Jones, C. S. Parnell, Charles Bradlaugh, and other advanced reformers. It is the kind of language which reformers expect from the Press, and also, I am sorry to say, from the Church. It is the natural language of shallow, or timid, or interested people, who are startled by the dreadful apparition of a new idea.

The agitator is not a nice man. He disturbs the general calm; he shakes old and rotten institutions with a rude hand; he drags into the light of day some loathsome and dangerous abuse which respectable rascality or cowardly conservatism has carefully covered up and concealed under a film of humbug. He tramples upon venerable shams; he injures old-established reputations; he bawls out shameful truths from the house-tops; he is fierce and noisy; uses strong language, and very often in his rage against wrong, or in the heat of his grief over unmerited suffering, he mixes his own truth with error, and carries his righteous denunciations to the point of injustice. The privileged classes hate him; the oppressed classes do not understand him; the lazy classes shun him as a pest. He finds himself standing, like Ishmael, with every man's hand against him.

Oliver Wendell Holmes compares the dawning of a new idea to the turning over of a stone in a field. After describing all the blind and wriggling creatures who live beneath the stone, he says:—

But no sooner is the stone turned and the wholesome light of day let in upon this compressed and blinded community of creeping things, than all of them which enjoy the luxury of legs—and some of them have a good many—rush round wildly, butting each other and everything in their way, and end in a general stampede for underground retreats from the region poisoned by sunshine. . . . You never need think you can turn over any old falsehood without a terrible squirming and scattering of the horrid little population that dwells under it.

Every real thought on every real subject knocks the wind out of somebody or other. As soon as his breath comes back he very probably begins to expend it in hard words. These are the best evidences a man can have that he has said something it was time to say.

But though the agitator is not a nice man, he is a useful man. Your pleasant, cultured, courteous, easy gentleman *is* a nice man, but he is the unconscious upholder of all that is bad, as well as of a little that is good.

There was a time, John, when women were tortured for witchcraft; when prisoners were tortured into the confession of crimes of which they were innocent; when good men and women were burnt alive for being unable to believe the dogmas of other men's religion; when authors had their ears cut off for telling the truth; when English children were worked to death in the factories; when starving workmen were hanged for stealing a little food; when boards of capitalists and landlords fixed the workers' wages; when Trade Unionism was conspiracy, and only rich men had votes. Those days are gone; those crimes are impossible; those wrongs are abolished. And for these changes we have to thank the agitators.

The agitators, John, from Christ downwards, have been the salt of the earth. It is only such as they who save society from dry rot and putrefaction.

Then, again, there is the practical hardheaded man, who always comes forward to prove every new thing impossible. John, we English have done many impossible things. Was it not demonstrated to the general satisfaction of the hard-headed ones that Stephenson could not make a train to go twelve miles an hour? Was it not proved that railways would exterminate horses? Was it not proved that the Atlantic cable could not be laid? Was it not made manifest that the Catholic Emancipation Acts, the Ballot Act, the Factory Acts, and the Repeal of the Corn Laws would plunge the nation into Popery, and anarchy, and ruin? Yet all these reforms were accomplished by little bands of agitators, in the face of tremendous opposition, and in spite of yells of execration, and virulent charges of "battening" and "incendiarism."

To return to our own time. There were never any men more virulently assailed than are the present leaders of the Labour movemen. The favourite lie is the charge of charlatanism. The man who conducts a strike or organises a trade union is alluded to by the Press as a "paid agitator"; the Labour paper is accused of "battening on the earnings of ignorant dupes."

When a paper calls a man a paid agitator, what does the charge imply? It implies that he is a liar and a rogue, who is preaching what he knows to be false, and preaching it for the sake of making money. So when a writer is accused of battening on the earnings of ignorant dupes, he is accused of wilfully gulling poor men for the sake of profit.

Such charges are uttered and reiterated with such malicious persistence, that thousands of worthy people have come to believe that the "paid agitator" has an easy and lucrative trade, and that the Labour paper is rolling in ill-gotten wealth as the result of its deliberate treachery to the poor.

Now, I will simply confront the slanders with the facts.

If Labour leaders were dull and incapable men, who could not hope to make money and position except as demagogues; if the work of the "paid agitator" were easy, and showed no signs of zeal and talent; if the "paid agitator" and the Labour writer preached only to ignorant people, if they preached doctrines which could not be maintained against the cleverest and best-informed leaders of the parties of privilege and plunder, if the salaries of the "paid agitators" and the "Labour writers" were high and their lives luxurious and easy, then there might be as much ground to suspect the *bonâ fides* of these men as there now is to suspect the *bonâ fides* of professional patriots, and of pressmen, who are bound by the tenets of their agreements always to prove Mr. Gladstone in the right, or always to prove him in the wrong.

But if "paid agitators" and Labour writers are proved to be men of industry and ability, who choose the thorny path instead of the flowery one; if their doctrines can withstand successfully all the attacks of their enemies; if they can be shown to be living sparely, working hard and earning very little, then it seems to me it will be unnecessary to defend their honour against the furtive slanders of nameless and incompetent writers who *are* well paid, and who *do* sell their consciences in the open market, and to the highest bidder.

It is a very effective picture, that of the paid agitator feasting on champagne and turtle, or of the Labour writer driving his carriage along the Brighton promenade. But it has the fault common to Press pictures—it is a *lie*.

Let us begin with the paid agitator. Is the trade so easy? Is it so well paid? Take John Burns. He is an engineer. Being a good workman John Burns could earn two pounds a week easily, and not work more than fifty-five hours. Now, I don't believe John has averaged two pounds a week as a Labour leader; and his wages have not been promptly paid; and I can remember an appeal for subscriptions to raise his present income of one pound a week, paid by the Dockers' Union, to two pounds; while as far as work is concerned his labour is endless and his working hours are *all* the hours he can spare from sleep.

The first time I saw him was during the Glasgow strike. He had made five long speeches that day. He was so hoarse that I could hardly hear him speak. He looked utterly fagged out, and at night he went to a second-rate temperance hotel and had weak tea and bread and butter for supper. This is not so fine a picture as the other; but it is *true*.

A paid agitator gets hard work, low pay, ingratitude, and vilification. He will be an old man before his time; but a rich man never. So much for the paid agitator. Now as to the Labour papers. We are confronted with the assertion that we batten on the earnings of misguided dupes. The men who write for the party papers do not batten on the misguided dupes. The rank and file of the political parties are *not* dupes. They are intelligent and discerning men. The writers on the party press are not hireling hacks. They are honourable men. It is merely a coincidence that their consciences always happen to fit in with the exigencies of the Liberal or Tory situation. They are quite different from the Labour writer. He "panders to the mob." He "battens on the foolish." He rolls in illgotten wealth.

Well; let some of the superior pressmen try it. Let them seek out the "dupes" and go in for "battening." They will find that the "dupe" does not yield much "batten" to the square inch. They will very soon have cause to sing the song of the disappointed Pirate—

> We boiled Bill Jones in the negro-pot,
> To see how much fat Bill Jones had got,
> But there wasn't much fat upon Jones.

To prove that all Labour writers are honest and earnest men may be difficult; but to prove that the British workman is not in the habit of bestowing his money on Labour leaders and Labour writers is *quite* easy.

Does the Labour journalist wallow in the wages of the worker? The devil a wallow. You leave that to the worker. He has money for beer, he has money for betting, he has money for parsons, he has money for missionaries, he has money for party politics, but he does *not* like his champions and his servants to get fat and lazy, and he takes precious good care they *don't*.

Proofs? Certainly. In bulk. No Labour paper ever yet paid its way. No Socialistic paper ever paid its way. There is not a single Labour leader, nor a single Labour writer in England to-day who is getting one-half the wages he could earn if he turned his back on Socialism for ever, and went in for making money. Not *one*.

Mr. Cunninghame Graham is a Labour leader. I don't suppose he ever made a five-pound note out of the cause. I *know* he has spent above a hundred five-pound notes, besides his time, in the cause.

Mr. de Mattos is a Fabian lecturer. He spends his whole time in lecturing on Socialism. He never gets a penny of pay.

Mr. Charles Bradlaugh was literally crushed to death, *killed* by debts contracted in fighting the battles of the democracy. The democracy let him die.

None of these men seem to have wallowed very deep in the earnings of their "dupes." But I hear that the *Times* and the *Telegraph* pay their writers well. *Comic Cuts* and the *Police News* are making fortunes. Messrs. Gladstone, Goschen, Salisbury, and Balfour get a decent living as politicians, and I have no doubt that Mr. Schnadhorst receives a better salary than John Burns.

There is nothing pays an English paper better than racing reports, betting tips, and prurient details of divorce trials. A Socialist paper will not stoop to any of these dirty ways of making money.

I commend these facts to the dailies. *They* write articles against gambling and print the tips, the betting, and the stock and share lists. They are honourable men.

If any of our readers have an idea that Socialism is a paying trade, I hope they will do us the justice to abandon that idea at once. Socialism is in its infancy as a cause. Socialism is not popular. The Socialists are few in number. Twenty years hence all this will be changed, and then the dailies will discover that early Socialists, though crude thinkers, were useful in preparing the public mind for the great utterances of the press. In fact, we are preparing the ground for the harvest which other men shall reap. So mote it be.

The Pope calls the pioneers of Socialism "crafty agitators." That word crafty implies that these "agitators" are seeking their own ends. I know many Socialists, and many Socialistic leaders. I know none who can make profit of it. *Most* of the leaders, such as Ruskin, Morris, Hyndman, Carpenter, Shaw, De Mattos, Annie Besant, and Bland, would lose in money and position were Socialism adopted now.

We Socialists don't complain about these things, but we respectfully submit the evidence to the jury, and ask for a verdict of acquittal on the charge of "Battening." We claim that we give our time and strength to the poor, and that we get but little in return but suspicion, and envy, and slander. God bless the poor, say I, and pity them. They are hard taskmasters, and as thankless as they are foolish, but they cannot help it, poor creatures, and we hope to do them good.

CHAPTER XXVI.

BEING a practical man, John, you will naturally say to me that having told you what I believe to be the true solution of the Social Problem, I ought to show some plan for working that solution out. I think, John, that the best way to realise Socialism is—to make Socialists. I have always maintained that if we can once get the people to understand how much they are wronged we may safely leave the remedy in their own hands. My work is to teach Socialism, to get recruits for the Socialist Army. I am not a general, but a recruiting sergeant. The most useful thing you can do is to join the recruiting staff yourself, and enlist as many volunteers as possible. Give us a Socialistic People, and Socialism will accomplish itself.

However, I may as well say a few words on the subject of Labour representation. The old struggles have been for political emancipation. The coming struggle will be for industrial emancipation. We want England for the English. We want the fruits of labour for those who produce them. This issue is not an issue between Liberals and Tories, it is an issue between Labourers and Capitalists. Neither of the Political Parties is of any use to the workers, because both the Political Parties are paid, officered and led by Capitalists whose interests are opposed to the interests of the workers. The Socialist laughs at the pretended friendship of Liberal and Tory leaders for the workers. These Party Politicians do not in the least understand what the rights, the interests, or the desires of the workers are; if they did understand they would oppose them implacably. The demand of the Socialist is a demand for the nationalisation of the land and all other instruments of production and distribution. The Party leaders will not hear of such a thing. If you want to get an idea how utterly destitute of sympathy with Labour the present House of Commons is, just read the reports of the speeches made on the occasions when Keir Hardie opposed the vote of congratulation on the Royal marriage, or when he and other Labour members raised the question of the employment of troops at Hull; or notice the attitude of the Party Press towards Socialism, Trade Unionism, Independent Labour Candidates, and the leaders of strikes. It is a very common thing to hear a Party Leader deprecate the increase of "class representation." What does that mean? It means Labour representation. But the

                      MERRIE ENGLAND.

"class" concerned in Labour representation is the working class, a "class" of some twenty-seven millions of people. Observe the calm effrontery of this sneer at "class representation." The twenty-seven millions of workers are not represented by more than a dozen members. The other classes—the landlords, the capitalists, the military, the law, the brewers, and idle gentlemen—are represented by something like six hundred and fifty members. This is class representation with a vengeance.

And mind you, John, this disproportion exists not only in Parliament, but in all county and municipal institutions. How many working men are there on the County Councils, the Boards of Guardians, the School Boards, and the Town Councils?

The Capitalists, and their hangers-on, not only make the laws—they administer them. Is it any wonder, then, that laws are made and administered in the interests of the Capitalist? And does it not seem reasonable to suppose that if the laws were made and administered by workers they would be made and administered to the advantage of Labour?

Well, my advice to you working men is to return working men representatives, with definite and imperative instructions, to Parliament and to all other governing bodies.

Some of the old Trade Unionists will tell you, John, that there is no need for Parliamentary interference in Labour matters. The Socialist does not ask for "Parliamentary interference," he asks for Government by the people and for the people.

The older unionists think that Trade Unionism is strong enough in itself to secure the rights of the worker. This is a great mistake. The rights of the worker are the whole of the produce of his Labour. Trade Unionism not only cannot secure that, but has never even tried to secure that. The most that Trade Unionism has secured, or can ever hope to secure for the workers, is a comfortable subsistence wage. They have not always secured even that much, and, when they have secured it, the cost has been serious. For the great weapon of Unionism is a strike, and a strike is at best a bitter, a painful, and a costly thing.

Do not think that I am opposed to Trade Unionism. It is a good thing; it has long been the only defence of the workers against robbery and oppression; were it not for the Trade Unionism of the past and of the present, the condition of the British industrial classes would be one of abject slavery. But Trade Unionism, although some defence, is not sufficient defence.

You must remember, also, that the employers have copied the methods of Trade Unionism. They also have organised and united, and in the future strikes will be more terrible and more costly than ever.

The Capitalist, John, is the stronger. He holds the better strategic position. He can always outlast the worker, for the worker has to starve and see his children starve, and the Capitalist never gets to that pass. Besides, capital is more mobile than labour. A stroke of the pen will divert wealth and trade from one end of the country to the other; but the workers cannot move their forces so readily.

One difference between Socialism and Trade Unionism is that whereas the Unions can only marshal and arm the workers for a desperate trial of endurance, Socialism can get rid of the Capitalist altogether. The former helps you to resist the enemy, the latter destroys him.

I suggest to you, John, that you should join a Socialist Society and help to get others to join, and that you should send Socialist workers to sit upon all representative bodies.

The Socialist tells you that you are men, with men's rights, and with men's capacities for all that is good and great—and you hoot him and call him a liar and a fool.

The Politician despises you, declares that all your sufferings are due to your own vices, that you are incapable of managing your own affairs, and that if you were entrusted with freedom and the use of the wealth you create you would degenerate into a lawless mob of drunken loafers—and you cheer him till you are hoarse.

The Politician tells you that *his* party is the people's party, and that *he* is the man to defend your interests, and in spite of all you know of his conduct in the past you believe him.

The Socialist begs you to form a party of your own, and to do your work yourself, and you write him down a knave.

To be a Trade Unionist and fight for your class during a strike, and to be a Tory or a Liberal and fight against your class at an election is folly.

During a strike there are no Tories or Liberals amongst the strikers; they are all workers. At election times there are no workers; only Liberals and Tories.

During an election there are Tory and Liberal Capitalists, and all of them are friends of the workers. During a strike there are no Tories and no Liberals amongst the employers. They are all Capitalists and enemies of the workers.

Is there any logic in you, John Smith? Is there any perception in you? Is there any sense in you?

You never elect an employer as president of a Trades Council; or as chairman of a Trade Union Congress; or as member of a Trade Union. You never ask an employer to lead you during a strike. But at election times, when you ought to stand by your class, the whole body of Trade Union workers turn into blacklegs, and fight for the Capitalist and against the workers.

I know that many of these Party Politicians are very plausible men, and that they protest very eloquently that their party really means to do well for the workers. But to those protests there is one unanswerable reply. Even if these men are as honest and as zealous as they pretend to be, I suppose you are not gullible enough to believe that they will do your work as well as you can do it yourselves.

I say to you, then, once more, John Smith, that the most practical thing you can do is to erase the words Liberal and Tory from your vocabulary, write Socialist in the place, and resolve that henceforward you will elect only Labour Representatives, and *see that they do their duty.*

CHAPTER XXVII.

IN answer to the common sneer that Socialists are insignificant, or unintelligent, or interested persons, I propose to give here a few brief extracts from men whose names are a sufficient guarantee of their own worthiness, and of the value of anything they say.

I shall begin by quoting John Stuart Mill, because he is a favourite authority with our opponents. He is a favourite authority of theirs, not because they have read him, for evidently they have not, but because he is generally regarded as a respectable and practical person.

John Stuart Mill says:—

The requisites of production are two: Labour, and appropriate natural objects.

Nothing here about the necessity for a capitalist. But again:—

It will be observed that I have assumed that the labourers are always subsisted from capital, and this is obviously the fact, although the capital needs not necessarily be furnished by a person called a capitalist.

Some obtuse persons have described capital as "the wages of abstinence." Mill says:—

In a rude and violent state of society it continually happens that the person who has capital is not the very person who has saved it, but someone who, being stronger, or belonging to a more powerful community, has possessed himself of it by plunder. And even in a state of things several degrees more advanced, the increase of capital has been in a great measure derived from privations which, though essentially the same with saving, are not generally called by that name, because not voluntary. The actual producers have been slaves, compelled to produce as much as force could extort from them, and to consume as little as self-interest, or the usually very slender humanity of their task-masters would permit.

I have frequently pointed out, Mr. Smith, that if wealth or capital is "the wages of abstinence," it is the wages of the abstinence of somebody else. That is to say, the so-called "thrift" of the capitalist is really *theft.*

The following lines of Mill bear rather heavily upon the absurd theory of "over-production":—

Thus the limit of wealth is never deficiency of consumers, but of producers and productive power.

These statements, John, merely convey facts which any man of sense must discover for himself. But then the people upon whom *you* rely for guidance, the politicians and press-men, are not men of sense.

Let us now turn from John Stuart Mill to Sir Thomas More. The following extracts are from Utopia :—

When I balance all these things in my thoughts, I grow more favourable to Plato, and do not wonder that he resolved not to make any laws for such as would not submit to a community of all things ; for so wise a man could not but foresee that the setting all upon a level was the only way to make a nation happy, which cannot be obtained so long as there is property ; for when every man draws to himself all that he can compass by one title or another, it must needs follow that how plentiful soever a nation may be, yet a few dividing the wealth of it among themselves, the rest must fall into indigence. So that there will be two sorts of people among them who deserve that their fortunes should be interchanged, the former useless, but wicked and ravenous, and the latter, who by their constant industry serve the public more than themselves, sincere and modest men. From whence I am persuaded that till property is taken away there can be no equitable or just distribution of things, nor can the world be happily governed ; for so long as that is maintained the greatest and the far best part of mankind will be still oppressed with a load of cares and anxieties.

Now comes Henry George :—

How contempt of human rights is the essential element in building up the great fortunes whose growth is such a marked feature of our development we have already seen. And just as clearly may we see that from the same cause spring poverty and pauperism. The tramp is the complement of the millionaire.

Read very carefully the following. It is from "The Story of My Heart," by Richard Jefferies—a beautiful book, John :—

This our earth this day produces sufficient for our existence, this our earth produces not only a suffi-ciency but a superabundance, and pours a cornucopia of good things down upon us. Further, it produces sufficient for stores and granaries to be filled to the roof-tree for years ahead. I verily believe that the earth in one year produces enough food to last for thirty. Why, then, have we not enough ? Why do people die of starvation, or lead a miserable existence on the verge of it ? Why have millions upon millions to toil from morning to evening just to gain a mere crust of bread ? Because of the absolute lack of organisation by which such labour should produce its effect, the absolute lack of distribution, the absolute lack, even, of the very idea that such things are possible. Nay, even to mention such things, to say that they are possible, is criminal with many. Madness could hardly go farther.

Now hear Joseph Mazzini :—

Many, too many, of you are poor. Life, for at least three-fourths of the working class, whether labourers or mechanics, is a daily struggle to obtain the *indis-pensable* material means of existence. They are occupied in manual labour for ten, twelve, sometimes fourteen hours a day, and by this constant, monoto-nous, and painful industry, they scarcely gain the bare necessaries of physical existence. The attempt to teach such men the duty of progress, to speak to them of their intellectual and moral life, of their political rights, or of education, is sheer irony in the present state of things.

And again :—

When society shall recognise no other distinction between *producers* and *consumers*; or rather, when every man shall be alike—producer and consumer ; when the profits of labour, instead of being parcelled out among that series of *intermediates*—which (be-ginning with the capitalist and ending with the retailer) frequently increases the price of production 50 per cent.—shall belong entirely to those who perform the labour, all the *permanent* causes of your poverty will be removed.

Emerson says :—

I would not have the labourer sacrificed to the result. I would not have the labourer sacrificed to my convenience and pride, nor to that of a great class of such as me. Let there be worse cotton and better men. The weaver should not be bereaved of his superiority to his work.

Compare this with Thorold Rogers :—

The people live in squalid dens, where there can be no health and no hope, but dogged discontent at their own lot, and futile discontent at the wealth which they see possessed by others.

Says Carlyle :—

The practice of modern Parliaments, with reporters sitting among them, and twenty-seven millions, mostly fools, listening to them, fills me with amazement.

On the subject of greatness Matthew Arnold says :—

If England were swallowed up by the sea to-morrow, which of the two, a hundred years hence, would most excite the love, interest, and admiration of mankind—would most, therefore, show the evi-dences of having possessed greatness—the England of the last twenty years, or the England of Elizabeth, of a time of splendid spiritual effort, but when our coal, and our industrial operations depending on coal, were very little developed ?

Compare this with Whitman :—

The place where a great city stands is not the place of stretched wharves, docks, manufactures, deposits of produce merely,

Nor the place of ceaseless salutes of new-comers, or the anchor-lifters of the departing,

Nor the place of the tallest and costliest buildings, or shops, selling goods from the rest of the earth,

Nor the place of the best libraries and schools, nor the place where money is plentiest,

Nor the place of the most numerous population.
Where the city stands with the brawniest breed of
orators and bards,
Where the city stands that is beloved by these, and
loves them in return and understands them,
Where no monuments exist to heroes but in the
common words and deeds,
Where thrift is in its place, and prudence is in its
place,
Where the men and women think lightly of the laws,
Where the slave ceases, and the master of slaves
ceases,
Where the populace rise at once against the never-
ending audacity of elected persons,
Where fierce men and women pour forth as the sea
to the whistle of death pours its sweeping and un-
rippled waves,
Where outside authority enters always after the
precedence of inside authority,
Where the citizen is always the head and ideal, and
the president, mayor, governor, and what not, are
agents for pay,
Where children are taught to be laws to themselves,
and to depend on themselves,
Where equanimity is illustrated in affairs,
Where speculations on the soul are encouraged,
Where women walk in public processions in the
streets the same as the men,
Where they enter the public assembly and take
places the same as the men;
Where the city of the faithfulest friends stands,
Where the city of the cleanliness of the sexes
stands,
Where the city of the healthiest fathers stands,
Where the city of the best-bodied mothers stands.
There the great city stands.

Read next this extract from Thoreau:—

Most men, even in this comparatively free country,
through mere ignorance and mistake, are so occupied with factitious cares and superfluously coarse
labours of life that its finer fruits cannot be plucked
by them. Their fingers, from excessive toil, are too
clumsy and tremble too much for that. Actually, the
labouring man has not leisure for a true integrity day
by day; he cannot afford to sustain the manliest relations to me; his labour would be depreciated in the
market. He has no time to be anything but a
machine. How can he remember well his ignorance—
which his growth requires—who has so often to
use his knowledge? We should feed and clothe
him gratuitously sometimes, and recruit him with
our cordials before we judge of him. The finest
qualities of our nature, like the bloom on fruits, can
be preserved only by the most delicate handling. Yet
we do not treat ourselves nor one another thus
tenderly.

And again:—

It is very evident what mean and sneaking lives
many of you live, for my sight has been whetted by
experience; always on the limits, trying to get into
business and trying to get out of debt, a very ancient
slough, called by the Latins *aes alienum*, another's

brass, for some of their coins were made of brass;
still living, and dying, and buried by this other's brass;
always promising to pay, promising to pay to-morrow,
and dying to-day insolvent; seeking to curry favour, to
get custom, by how many modes—only not state-
prison offences: lying, flattering, voting, contracting
yourselves into a nutshell of civility, or dilating into
an atmosphere of thin and vaporous generosity,
that you may persuade your neighbour to let you
make his shoes, or his hat, or his coat, or his carriage,
or import his groceries for him; making yourselves
sick that you may lay up something against a sick
day, something to be tucked away in an old chest or
in a stocking behind the plastering, or more safely in
the brick bank, no matter where, no matter how
much or how little.

And now, John, steady yourself, for it is
going to thunder. That is to say, I am going
to quote Carlyle:

True, it must be owned, we for the present, with
our Mammon-Gospel, have come to strange conclusions. We call it a Society; and go about professing
openly the totalest separation, isolation. Our life is
not a mutual helpfulness; but rather, cloaked under
due laws of war, named "fair competition," and so
forth, it is a mutual hostility. We have profoundly
forgotten everywhere that *cash-payment* is not the
sole relation of human beings; we think, nothing
doubting, that *it* absolves and liquidates all engage-
ments of man. "My starving workers?" answers
the rich mill-owner: "Did I not hire them fairly in
the market? Did I not pay them, to the last sixpence, the sum covenanted for? What have I to do
with them more?" Verily, Mammon-worship is a
melancholy creed. When Cain, for his own behoof,
had killed Abel, and was questioned, "Where is thy
brother?" he too made answer, "Am I my brother's
keeper?" Did I not pay my brother *his* wages, the
thing he had merited from me? . . .
Did William the Norman Bastard, or any of his
Taillefers, *Ironcutters*, manage so? Ironcutter, at
the end of the campaign, did not turn off his thousand fighters, but said to them: "Noble fighters, this
is the land we have gained; be I Lord in it—what we
will call *Law-ward*, maintainer and *keeper* of Heaven's
Laws: be I *Law-ward*, or in brief orthoepy, Lord in
it, and be ye Loyal Men around me in it; and we will
stand by one another as soldiers round a captain, for
again we shall have need of one another!" Plugson,
bucanier-like, says to them: "Noble spinners, this is
the Hundred Thousand we have gained, wherein I
mean to dwell and plant vineyards; the hundred
thousand is mine, the three and sixpence daily was
yours: adieu, noble spinners; drink my health with
this groat each, which I give you over and above!"
The entirely unjust Captain of Industry, say I; not
Chevalier, but Bucanier! . . . A human being who
has worked with human beings clears all scores with
them, cuts himself with triumphant completeness
forever loose from them, by paying down certain
shillings and pounds. Was it not the wages I promised
you? There they are to the last sixpence,—according

to the laws of the Bucaniers—yes indeed—and at such times it becomes imperatively necessary to ask all persons, Bucaniers and others, whether these same respectable Laws of the Bucaniers are written on God's eternal Heavens at all, on the Inner Heart of Man at all; or on the respectable Bucanier Logbook merely, for the convenience of Bucaniering merely? What a question—whereat Westminster Hall shudders to its driest parchment; and on the dead wigs each particular horsehair stands on end! . . .

Supply-and-demand,——Alas! for what noble work was there ever yet any audible "demand" in that poor sense? The man of Macedonia speaking in vision to an Apostle Paul, "Come over and help us," did not specify what rate of wages he would give! Or was the Christian Religion itself accomplished by Prize Essays, Bridgewater Bequests, and a "minimum of four thousand five hundred a year"? No demand that I heard of was made them, audible in any Labour Market, Manchester Chamber of Commerce, or other the like emporium and hiring establishment; silent were all these from any whisper of such demand; powerless were all these to "supply it" had the demand been in thunder and earthquake, with gold El Dorados and Mahometan Paradises for the reward. Ah me, into what waste latitudes in this Time-Voyage have we wandered, like adventurous Sinbads; where the men go about as if by galvanism, with meaningless glaring eyes, and have no soul, but only of the beaver faculty and stomach! The haggard despair of Cotton Factory, coal mine operatives, Chandos Farm labourers, in these days is painful to behold; but not so painful, hideous to the inner sense, as that brutish God-forgetting profit-and-loss Philosophy and Life-theory, which we hear jangled on all hands of us, in senate-houses, spouting clubs, leading articles, pulpits and platforms, everywhere as the Ultimate Gospel and candid plain-English of Man's Life, from the throats and pens and thoughts of all-but all men!

Enlightened philosophies, like Molière doctors, will tell you: " Enthusiasms, self-sacrifice, Heaven, Hell, and such like; yes, all that is true enough for old stupid times; all that used to be true; but we have changed all that, *nous avons changé tout cela!*" Well, if the heart be got round now into the right side and the liver to the left; if man have no heroism in him deeper than the wish to eat, and in his soul there dwell now no Infinite of Hope and Awe, and no Divine Silence can become imperative because it is not Sinai Thunder, and no tie will bind if it be not that of Tyburn gallows-ropes—then verily you have changed all that; and for it, and for you, and for me, the Abyss and nameless Annihilation is ready. So scandalous a beggarly Universe deserves, indeed, nothing else; I cannot say I would save it from annihilation. Vacuum, and the Serene Blue, will be much handsomer, easier, too, for all of us. I, for one, decline living as a Patent-Digester, Spinning-Mule, Mayfair clothes-horse ; many thanks, but your Chaosships will have the goodness to excuse me !

Cicero says :—

One thing ought to be aimed at by all men; that the interest of each individually, and of all collectively, should be the same; for if each should grasp at his individual interest, all human society will be dissolved.

In the book of Isaiah occurs a passage which seems like a description of Commercial England :—

Their land also is full of silver and gold, neither is there any end of their treasures; their land also is full of horses, neither is there any end of their chariots. Their land also is full of idols : they worship the work of their own hands, that which their own fingers have made.

A little farther on in the same book we have this fine passage :—

The Lord will enter into judgment with the elders of His people. It is ye that have eaten up the vine-yard; the spoil of the poor is in your houses; what mean ye that ye crush My people, and grind the faces of the poor? saith the Lord, the Lord of Hosts.

De Balzac says :—

Morality and political economy unite in repelling the individual who consumes without producing.

Christ said :—

It is easier for a camel to pass through a needle's eye than for a rich man to enter the Kingdom of Heaven.

With such quotations, Mr. Smith, taken from the writings of men of probity and genius, I could easily fill a volume. Instead, I will give you a list of the books wherein you may find them for yourself. I hope you will read them, if only to correct the evil effects of a long course of newspaper twaddle and oratorical fustian.

This question of Socialism is the most important and imperative question of the age. It will divide, is now dividing, society into two camps. In which camp will you elect to stand? On the one side there are individualism and competition—leading to a "great trade" and great miseries. On the other side is justice, without which can come no good, from which can come no evil. On the one hand are ranged all the sages, all the saints, all the martyrs, all the noble manhood and pure womanhood of the world; on the other hand are the tyrant, the robber, the manslayer, the libertine, the usurer, the slave-driver, the drunkard, and the sweater. Choose your party, then, my friend, and let us get to the fighting.

CHAPTER XXVIII.

WHEN I began these letters, Mr. Smith, I promised to put the case for Socialism before you as clearly and as plainly as I could, asking you in return to render a verdict in accordance with the evidence.

I have now done the work as well as I could under the circumstances; and I leave the matter in your hands.

"Merrie England" is not as lucid, nor as strong, nor as complete as I hoped to make it, but it may serve to suggest the wisdom of wider studies.

A good work of this kind has long been needed. I have not had time, nor health, nor opportunity to do it thoroughly, but I thought it better to do it as well as I could than to wait until I could take a whole year in which to do it more thoroughly.

Perhaps some day I will set to work and do it all over again. Meanwhile I ask you to believe that there is a great deal more to be said for Socialism than these papers of mine contain, and I suggest to you that it would be well to read the books I have recommended; firstly because knowledge is always valuable, and secondly because it is your duty as a man and a citizen to understand the society you live in, and to mend it if you can.

There are very many well-meaning people who, whilst owning that much wrong and misery exist, deny their own responsibility for any part of them.

Very commonly we hear men say, "Yes, it is a pity that things are so bad; but it is no fault of ours, and nothing we can do will mend them."

Now, John, that is a cowardly and dishonest excuse. It is the old plea of Cain, "Am I my brother's keeper?" No one can shirk his responsibility. We are none of us guiltless when wrong is done. We are all responsible in some degree for every crime and sin, and for every grief and shame for which or by which our fellow creatures suffer.

If, for instance, the filthy condition of the Salford Docks should cause sickness and loss of life, every citizen from the highest to the lowest would be responsible for the wrong.

When injustice is done it avails not for a man to plead that he cannot prevent it. The fact is he has not *tried* to prevent it, and therein lies his sin.

The average citizen sees the slums and the sweaters; he sees the wretched and the destitute; he knows that the weak and innocent are systematically robbed and slain; and his one excuse is that he "cannot help it." Now, John, I ask *you*, have you *tried* to help it; or have you only lied to yourself by saying no help was possible?

Your duty, it seems to me, is clear enough. First of all, having seen that misery and wrong exist, it is your duty to find out *why* they exist. Having found out why they exist, it is your duty to seek for means to abolish them. Having found out the means to abolish them, it is your duty to apply these means, or, if you have not yourself the power, it is your duty to persuade others to help you.

Do your duty, John. Do not lie to your soul any more. Long have you known that injustice and misery are rife amongst the people. If you have not acted upon the knowledge it is not because you knew it to be useless so to act, but because you were lazy and preferred your ease, or because you were selfish and feared to lose your own advantage, or because you were heartless and did not really feel any pang at sight of the sufferings of others.

Let us have the *truth*, John, howsoever painful it may be; let us have *justice*, no matter what the cost.

Go out into the streets of any big English town, and use your eyes, John. What do you find? You find some rich and idle, wasting unearned wealth to their own shame and injury and the shame and injury of others. You find hard-working people packed away in vile, unhealthy streets. You find little children famished, dirty, and half naked outside the luxurious clubs, shops, hotels, and theatres. You find men and women overworked and underpaid. You find vice and want and disease cheek by jowl with religion and culture and wealth. You find the usurer, the gambler, the fop, the finnikin fine lady, and you find the starveling, the slave, the vagrant, the drunkard, and the harlot.

Is it nothing to you, John Smith? Are you a citizen? Are you a man? And will not strike a blow for the right, nor lift a hand to save the fallen, nor make the smallest sacrifice for the sake of your brothers and your sisters!

John, I am not trying to work upon your feelings. This is not rhetoric, it is hard fact. Throughout these letters I have tried to be plain, and practical, and moderate. I have never so much as offered you a glimpse of the higher regions of thought. I have suffered no hint of idealism to escape me. I have kept as close to the earth as I could. I am only now talking street talk about the common sights of the common town. I say that wrong and sorrow are here crushing the life out of our brothers and sisters. I say that you, in common with all men, are responsible for the things that are. I say that it is your duty to seek the remedy; and I say that if you seek it you will find it.

These common sights of the common streets, John, are very terrible to me. To a man of a nervous temperament, at once thoughtful and imaginative, those sights must be terrible. The prostitute under the lamps, the baby beggar in the gutter, the broken pauper in his livery of shame, the weary worker stifling in his filthy slums, the wage slave toiling at his task, the sweater's victim "sewing at once, with a double thread, a shroud as well as a shirt," these are dreadful, ghastly, shameful facts which long since seared themselves upon my heart.

All this sin, all this wretchedness, all this pain, in spite of the smiling fields and the laughing waters, under the awful and unsullied sky. And no remedy!

These things I saw, and I knew that I was responsible as a man. Then I tried to find out the causes of the wrong and the remedy therefor. It has taken me some years, John. But I think I understand it now and I want you to understand it, and to help in your turn to teach the truth to others.

Sometimes while I have been writing these letters I have felt very bitter and very angry. More than once I have thought that when I had got through the work I would ease my heart with a few lines of irony or invective. But I have thought better of it. Looking back now I remember my own weakness, folly, cowardice. I have no heart to scorn or censure other men. Charity, John, mercy, John, humility, John. We are poor creatures, all of us.

So here is "Merrie England;" the earnest though weak effort of this poor clod of wayward marl, this little pinch of valiant dust. If it does good—well; if not—well. I will try again.

Also, some day, perhaps, I will talk to you not as a practical man, but as a human being. I will ask you to feel with me the pulsing of the universal heart, to see with me the awful eyes of the universal soul, gazing upward, dim and blurred and weary, but full of a wistful yearning for the unrevealed and unspeakable glory which men call God.

But these are "practical" letters, written with a practical object, and addressed to practical people. They are here republished as a book; and as they have cost me some time and trouble in the writing, I ask you, on your part, to give a little time and trouble to the reading, and, further, if, after that, you think them worth what they have cost you, I shall be glad if you will help me by recommending them to your friends.

APPENDIX.

I N case you should desire to go into these matters more fully, Mr. Smith, I recommend you to get Fabian Tract No. 29, "What to Read" (price threepence : Fabian Society, 276, Strand, W.C.). I should also advise you to read the following pamphlets, all of which can be got for one-and-sevenpence :—

1. Facts for Socialists..276, Strand 1d.
2. Capital and Land...276, Strand 1d.
3. Society Classified...W. Reeves, 185, Fleet-street 1d.
4. Simple Division..A. Heywood, Manchester 1d.
5. Mining Rents and Royalties...W. Reeves 1d.
6. Wage, Labour, and Capital...S.D.F., 337, Strand 2d.
7. Useful Work and Useless Toil.................................Hammersmith Socialist Society 1d.
8. True and False Society..Hammersmith Socialist Society 1d.
9. Rights of the Worker According to Ruskin.................................W. Reeves 1d.
10. The Law of Supply and Demand...........................Manchester Labour Press 1d.
11. Socialism Made Plain...S.D.F., 337, Strand 1d.
12. Milk and Postage Stamps..A. Heywood, Manchester 1d.
13. Constitutional Socialism..W. Reeves 3d.
14. The Pope's Socialism...Manchester Labour Press 1d.
15. The Socialist Catechism.............................W. Reeves, 185, Fleet-street 1d.
16. A King's Lesson..Hammersmith Socialist Society 1d.

I can also recommend the following books:—

			S.	D.
1. The Child's History of England...Dickens	Chapman and Hall	3	6
2. Hard Times...Dickens	Chapman and Hall	3	0
3. The Snob Papers...Thackeray	Smith, Elder	1	0
4. England's Ideal...Carpenter	Swan Sonnenschein	2	6
5. Whitman's Poems...Whitman	Walter Scott	1	0
6. Past and Present...Carlyle	Chapman and Hall	1	0
7. Latter-Day Pamphlets...Carlyle	Chapman and Hall	1	0
8. Our Old Nobility...Evans	Walter Vickars, Strand	1	0
9. Unto This Last...Ruskin	G. Allen, Orpington	5	0
10. Industrial History of England...Gibbins	Methuen	2	6
11. Walden...Thoreau	Walter Scott	1	6
12. Socialism Made Plain...Fairman	Wm. Reeves, Fleet-street	1	0
13. The Fabian Essays...Fabian Society	276, Strand	1	0
14. England for All...Hyndman	Social Democratic Federation	0	6
15. Ideal Commonwealths...Plato, More, Bacon, &c.	Routledge	1	6
16. News from Nowhere...Morris	Reeves and Turner	1	0
17. The Story of My Heart...Jefferies	Longmans and Co.	6	0
18. Dreams...Olive Schreiner		6	0

I recommend you to read the above works in the order in which I have placed them, because I think that you will then more fully enter into the spirit of "Merrie England," and will better comprehend the peculiarities of that peculiar paper, the *Clarion*.

I should, however, like you to read many other books besides those, and, amongst them, Cobbett's Grammar, Whately's "Logic," Eliot's "Silas Marner," Emerson's Essays, Dickens' "Tale of Two Cities" and Christmas Stories, and all the works of Ruskin (particularly "Fors Clavigera") and Carlyle. There are also a few poems: "Jenny," by D. G. Rossetti; "One Among so Many" and "Aux Ternes," from "Songs of the Army of the Night," by Francis Adams; "The Song of the Shirt," by Tom Hood; "The Cry of the Children," by Mrs. Browning; and "The Fourth Psalm," by Milton. And if you read, in "Fantasias," "My Sister" and "Bogeyland," I should not be offended. The fact is, John, I wish you to be a Clarionette as well as a Socialist.

INDEX.

The Journeyman Press

The Journeyman Press was set up towards the end of 1974 with the principal aim of keeping in print books which have come to be regarded as socialist 'classics'. Since then it has broadened its scope to include one or two original works. However, its purpose remains clear: *to publish books which reflect something of the struggles of working people in class society and, as such, have helped to strengthen the development of a socialist consciousness.*

SIX RED MONTHS IN RUSSIA by Louise Bryant (Ann Reed) 1919. The eye-witness report by John Reed's wife of revolutionary Russia. Illustrated, *paperback* £1.25

THE IRON HEEL by Jack London (1907). One of the most famous novels to influence Socialists throughout the World. *Paperback* 75p, *hardback* £2.50

SHELLEY'S SOCIALISM by Edward Aveling and Eleanor Marx Aveling (1888), with a Preface by Frank Allaun MP. A short but fascinating Marxist analysis of Shelley's poetry. *Limp* 60p

KARL MARX: Biographical Memoirs by Wilhelm Liebknecht (1901). Never reprinted before, but always quoted. Reminiscences of one of Marx's oldest friends. *Paperback* £1

FONTAMARA by Ignazio Silone (1934). The moving story of an Italian village's resistance to Fascism. *Paperback* 75p

THE GENERALS' STRIKE: Twenty drawings by Andrew Turner, with an Introduction by Ray Watkinson and a Foreword by Dai Francis. *An Original Journeyman* to be published Summer 1976. A unique series of drawings on the General Strike by one of Britain's few committed artists. Large format, *paperback* £1.50

CARTOONS FOR THE CAUSE by Walter Crane (1896), with a Foreword by John Betjeman, and published with the Marx Memorial Library, Summer 1976. Crane's most important drawings and poems for the Labour Movement around the turn of the century. Large format, *limp* £3. (*Numbers 1 to 100 limited*)

VICTORIA PARK: The Social History of an East End Park by Charles Poulsen, to be published Autumn 1976 with Stepney Books. *An Original Journeyman.* The first historical record of this famous meeting place for London's working class. Illustrated, *paperback* 90p

REVOLUTIONARY ACTS edited, with an Introduction and Epilogue, by Valerie Miner. *An Original Journeyman* to be published Autumn 1976. A valuable working study of street theatre in Britain since the sixties, including scripts by 7.84, Red Ladder, West London Theatre Workshop, Women's Theatre Group, and the Belts and Braces Roadshow. Illustrated, *paperback* £1.25

The Journeyman Press is also distributing a series of 'Chapbooks' published by *Oriole Editions* in New York. Unfortunately, because costings differ in the US from our own, the prices have to be higher than we would have liked. However, their value lies in their being unobtainable otherwise, hence the decision to distribute them:

THE STORY OF THE IRISH CITIZEN ARMY by Sean O'Casey 90p

THE CANTON SPEECH, SPEECHES TO COURT AND JURY
by Eugene V. Debs 50p

ON THE NATURE AND USES OF SABOTAGE by Thorstein
Veblen 40p

THE INDUSTRIAL SYSTEM AND THE CAPTAINS OF
INDUSTRY by Thorstein Veblem 40p

THE CASTAWAYS OF PLENTY: A Parable of Our Time by W. E.
Hawkins 75p

THE SOUL OF MAN UNDER SOCIALISM by Oscar Wilde 50p

A DREAM OF JOHN BALL by William Morris 65p

A PIECE OF CHALK by Thomas H. Huxley 35p

SOCIAL PHILOSOPHY AND THE AMERICAN SCENE *together
with* MATERIALISM AND HUMAN KNOWING by Roy Wood
Sellars 70p

FACING THE CHAIR: Sacco and Vanzetti. The story of the
Americanization of Two Foreign Born Workmen by John Dos
Passos £1

THE TEARS OF THE INDIANS by Bartolome de Las Casas.
Transcribed from the original edition of 1656 which was translated,
with an Epistolary Dedication to Oliver Cromwell, by John Phillips.
Now published with a new Historical Introduction by Colin Steele
of the Bodleian Library, Oxford University £1

CIVIL WAR IN WEST VIRGINIA: The story of the Industrial
Conflict in the Coal Mines by Winthrop D. Lane £1

AN ADDRESS TO THE IRISH PEOPLE by Percy Bysshe Shelley.
First published in Dublin in 1812 75p

Also by *Oriole Editions:*

HAMMER OR ANVIL: The Story of the German Working-Class Movement by Evelyn Anderson. First published in the UK in 1945. *Hardback*
£5.25

ART AND SOCIETY & Other Papers in Historical Materialism by George
V. Plekhanov. *Hardback* £5.25

The INTRODUCTIONS to the Collected Works of WILLIAM MORRIS
by May Morris, with a Preface by J. R. Dunlapp. *2 Volumes* £18

---

*If ordering any of these books please add approximately 20% to cover postage
and packing. Your order will be recorded if a title is not yet available, and
sent to you as soon as we have stocks.*

So that pamphlets could also be reprinted, the *Radical Reprint Club* was created in 1975/6. By printing against orders received, attractive hardback editions of famous – but very scarce – pamphlets can be reprinted at quite low prices, for what are effectively limited editions. During 1976 the first selection has included:

1. GRAND NATIONAL HOLIDAY, AND CONGRESS OF THE PRODUCTIVE CLASSES by William Benbow (1832). The first published hint that the general strike could be used as a political weapon.
2. ADDRESS TO THE TRADES' UNIONS, issued by the Council of the Socialist League (1885). *The Socialist Platform Series No. 1.*
3. USEFUL WORK vs. USELESS TOIL by William Morris (1885). *The Socialist Platform Series No. 2.*
4. THE RUSSIANS OF ROSS-SHIRE, OR MASSACRE OF THE ROSSES IN STRATHCANON, ROSS-SHIRE BY POLICEMEN, WHEN SERVING THE TENANTS IN STRATHCANON WITH SUMMONSES OF REMOVAL LAST MARCH by Donald Ross (1854). A vivid account of police brutality during the clearing of the Glens.

The second selection will include:
6. THE FACTORY HELL by Edward Aveling and Eleanor Marx Aveling (1885). *The Socialist Platform Series No. 3.*
7. A SHORT ACCOUNT OF THE COMMUNE OF PARIS by Ernest Belfort Bax, Victor Dane and William Morris (1886). *The Socialist Platform Series No. 4.*

For more details about *Journeyman* titles or the *Radical Reprint Club*, please write to the address below:

97 Ferme Park Road
Crouch End London N8 9SA